wild
SRI LANKA

wild SRI LANKA

Gehan de Silva Wijeyeratne

JOHN BEAUFOY PUBLISHING

Page 1: *A Peacock dances to attract a female to its harem in Yala.*

Pages 2 and 3: *The Elephant Gatherings in Minneriya and Kaudulla National Parks provide an amazing opportunity to observe social interactions between Asian Elephants in the wild.*

These pages, main picture: *The highland forests of Sri Lanka have been lost to plantations and only a precious few remain in reserves.*
Insets (opposite from top): *Pioneer butterfly; Ceylon Blue Magpie; Sambar; Rhododendron.*

Contents

Bay of Bengal
INDIA
Palk Strait
Kankasenturai
Jaffna
Karaitivu
Analaitivu
Nainativu
Kayts
Delft
Palk Bay
Jaffna Lagoon
Bay of Bengal
Devil's Point
Iranativu
Gulf of Mannar Biosphere Reserve
Adam's Bridge
Mannar Island
Talaimannar
Mannar
Talladi
NORTHERN
Mankulam
Mullaittivu
Vavuniya
INDIAN OCEAN
Pigeon Island
Nilaveli
Swami Rock
Trincomalee
China Bay
Foul Point
Horowupotana
Medawachchiya
Portugal Bay
Wilpattu National Park
Mihintale
Anuradhapura
Dutch Bay
Yan
Hurulu Nature Park
Gulf of Mannar
Kalpitiya
NORTH CENTRAL
Puttalam Lagoon
Kaudulla National Park
Ritigala Forest Reserve
Puttalam
NORTH WESTERN
Habarana
Giritale
Minneriya National Park
Minneriya Lake
Elephant Point
Sigiriya
Polonnaruwa
Passikudah
Dambulla
Kandalama
EASTERN
Eravur
Wasgomuwa National Park
Arachchikattuwa
Deduru Oya
Maduru Oya
Batticaloa
Chilaw
SRI LANKA
Kurunegala
Matale
KNUCKLES RANGE
Pinnawala
Kandy
Mahiyangana
Ampara
Peradeniya
Kandy Lake
Negombo
Kegalle
Katunayaka
SABARAGAMUWA
CENTRAL
WESTERN
Gampaha
Nuwara Eliya
Badulla
UVA
COLOMBO
Kotte
Adam's Peak
Hakgala Strict Nature Reserve
Lahugala
Pottuvil
Mount Lavinia
2243m
Ambewala
Pattipola
Moneragala
Moratuwa
Ohiya
Haputale
Bodhinagala
Horton Plains National Park
Arugam Bay
Panadura
Ratnapura
Wellawaya
Pelmadulla
Kalutara
Agalawatte
Yala National Park
Katukurunda
Kalawana
Uda Walawe National Park
Kumana
Beruwela
Timbolketiya
Sinharaja Man and Biosphere Reserve
Tanamalwila
Kataragama
Little Basses
Kosgoda
Elipitiya
Embilipitiya
Tissamaharama
Ambalangoda
Kanneliya Forest Reserve
Kirinda
Great Basses
Hikkaduwa
SOUTHERN
Bundala National Park
Kottawa
Hungama
Hambantota
Galle
Kottawa-Kombala Forest Reserve
Rekawa
Unawatuna
Tangalle
Mirissa
Matara
Weligama
Dondra Head
N
Mountains and hill peaks
Capital
City
Major town
Town or village
Provincial boundary
Main road
Minor road
Railway
River
Airport
National parks and reserves
0
50 km
0
50 miles
79
80
81
82
10
9
8
7
6

Preface

No word encapsulates my life and career better than 'serendipity', the finding of happy and unexpected discoveries by accident. The word itself derives from Serendip, a classical Arabic name for Sri Lanka. The island's plants and animals, it was thought, had been completely catalogued in the course of almost five centuries of colonial occupation. After all, Carolus Linnaeus himself had as long ago as 1747 written a detailed account of its flora. So when I and my colleagues at the Wildlife Heritage Trust of Sri Lanka began exploring Sri Lanka's forests in the late 1980s, we didn't really expect many surprises. Were we wrong! In the succeeding three decades we were to discover and describe more than 20 new species of freshwater fish, 45 amphibians, 25 reptiles, 40 freshwater crabs and even a couple of mammals, all of them endemic to Sri Lanka. Work continues on the description of many others.

Sri Lanka's biodiversity is indeed full of surprises, and that's not just in terms of numbers of species. As these pages show, it also offers some of the world's greatest wildlife spectacles, not least the breathtaking Asian Elephant Gathering and Sperm Whale super-pods. For an island of its size (65,000 sq km/25,000 sq miles, about the same as Tasmania) it packs more punch in terms of its wildlife than any other. Whether you are a twitcher anxiously ticking off the endemic birds on your list, a photographer in search of that prize-winning image, or a holidaymaker just in search of memories, Sri Lanka is your one-stop shop.

Visitors to Sri Lanka need to bear in mind, however, that the whole is greater than the sum of its parts. The island's species inventory is extensive, but not the world's biggest. Its share of big game is large, but not as large as Africa's. Its wilderness areas are wild, but there are wilder. Add all these up, however, and as Gehan points out, there is no place quite like it. As the poet Heber observed two centuries ago, 'its every prospect pleases'.

Remember also that Sri Lanka is a work in progress. Centuries of colonial rule followed by a three decade-long civil war (now over) and the devastating Boxing Day tsunami of 2004 have left their scars. Despite these setbacks, however, it is now on a path to rapid development. Though there have been fears for the well-being of its faunal and floral riches, the people's deeply rooted Buddhist traditions and the reverence this evokes for all life have paid a substantial conservation dividend.

No one has strived harder than Gehan de Silva Wijeyeratne to promote sustainable nature tourism in Sri Lanka. *Wild Sri Lanka* is a work of seduction. In it Gehan showcases through an informative text and a selection of outstanding photographs what you can expect to find here. By buying this book you have taken the first step.

Serendipity awaits.

Rohan Pethiyagoda

Rohan Pethiyagoda, an engineer and scientist, has with colleagues at the Wildlife Heritage Trust of Sri Lanka been responsible for the discovery and description of almost 150 new species in Sri Lanka. He has written many books on Sri Lanka's wildlife. He is a trustee of the International Trust for Zoological Nomenclature and has served as Deputy Chair of the IUCN's Species Survival Commission.

Foreword

I have travelled around the world to watch wildlife; sometimes on private visits, at other times on professional assignments on press trips or with film crews to make wildlife documentaries for television. Like many serious wildlife enthusiasts, I buy field guides to a country's wildlife. In Sri Lanka, I found there were many guide books available for various faunal groups, such as birds, butterflies and dragonflies, as well as books giving overviews of the wildlife of the country and its national parks and reserves. What struck me was that almost all of them seem to have been written by one person. This is Gehan de Silva Wijeyeratne. I have travelled to many countries and I do not think I have been to any country where a single individual has done as much as Gehan has done to publicize Sri Lanka's wildlife.

In November 2010 at the World Travel Market (WTM), I was asked to be the chief guest at the Sri Lanka stall at a press conference attended by the Chairman and Directors of the Sri Lanka Tourism Promotion Bureau. I spoke to the press about my recent press visit to Sri Lanka. I commented on the range and variety of literature brought out by Gehan and how every big wildlife story from the country has included his involvement.

Before and after my press trip to Sri Lanka, Gehan briefed me on the top Sri Lankan wildlife stories broken by him, and in particular on his claim that Sri Lanka is the best for big-game safaris outside Africa. More recently, in January 2013, he began a media campaign to explain why Sri Lanka has a strong claim to be the best all-round wildlife destination for its combination of big-game land animals, marine mammals and endemic biodiversity in a compact area, with the possibility of seeing the highlights both easily and affordably.

I am happy to see that Gehan's efforts to position Sri Lanka as a top wildlife destination are continuing. *Wild Sri Lanka* brings together all of the big wildlife stories from Sri Lanka, together with insights into what to look for in terms of behaviour, as well as when and where to see the animals and plants. It combines quality photography with accounts based on extensive first-hand familiarity within the field.

Bill Oddie

Bill Oddie is a wildlife expert specializing in birds and birdwatching. He was awarded the OBE (Officer of the Order of the British Empire) in 2003 for his services to wildlife conservation. He is also a broadcaster, actor and television presenter, as well as the author of numerous books on wildlife.

Above: *The Grey-headed Canary Flycatcher can be found in urban habitats in the hills if wooded patches are present. Its call is reminiscent of a Canary's.*

Opposite: *The steep ascent to Horton Plains National Park from the Pattipola side offers contrasting views of cloud forest with cycatheas and degraded highlands.*

1 Introduction

Sri Lanka inherited an interest in natural history as part of its British colonial legacy. As a result it has a fairly rich natural history literature, though in the last decade or so only a handful of books aimed at wildlife enthusiasts, giving overviews of its natural history, have been published. *Wild Sri Lanka* focuses on the terrestrial and marine wildlife, and the fantastic national parks where specific species can be seen.

Left: *Meethrigala is one of a few forest reserves with Buddhist hermitages that provide a refuge for endemic biodiversity in the densely populated west of the island.*

Naturalists, Past and Present

Sri Lanka has an ethnobotanical tradition with its own version of Ayurveda medicine (of Indian origin) which may go back over 2,000 years. However, there is very little on record of any studies of natural history in the modern sense by Sri Lankans until the 19th century, when E. F. Kelaart, born in Sri Lanka to parents of Dutch descent, published a series of works culminating in his *Prodromus Faunæ Zeylanicæ* (1852).

Modern natural history studies in Sri Lanka began with the 16th-century voyages of Europeans in search of trade, an outcome of which was the collection of specimens for cabinets of natural history curiosities that were being accumulated in the West. Colonization of Sri Lanka by the Portuguese was followed by that of the Dutch and British, and the last two nations in particular had a strong scientific interest in collecting specimens. So great was European interest in Sri Lanka's plants that the three decades between 1717 and 1747 saw the publication of three comprehensive floras, by Paul Hermann, Johannes Burman and the 'father' of botany himself, Carl Linnaeus. *Systema Naturae* (1758), Linnaeus's revolutionary work, included a number of the island's plants and animals. It introduced the binomial system of naming species that is still in use to this day.

Following the botanists came the zoologists anxious to describe Sri Lanka's fauna. Loten's Sunbird, for example, was among the many species named from drawings made for Gideon Loten, the Dutch colonial governor of the island from 1752 to 1757, who collected natural history specimens and also maintained a menagerie. The tradition of the publication of books for an audience of wildlife watchers was largely the work of British colonial naturalists, some of whom were planters or in the Ceylon Civil Service. Early writers included Sir James Emerson Tennent (*Sketches of the Natural History of Ceylon*, 1861), Captain Vincent W. Legge (*History of the Birds of Ceylon*, 1878–80), L. G. O. Woodhouse (*The Butterfly Fauna of Ceylon*, 1942) and G. M. Henry (*A Guide to the Birds of Ceylon*, 1955). For more on the early history of the discovery of Sri Lanka's biodiversity, see *Pearls, Spices and Green Gold* (2007) by Rohan Pethiyagoda.

Sri Lanka's flora and fauna were subject to collecting and scientific description by a number of European professional and amateur naturalists over a span of four centuries. Impetus was given to this enterprise with the establishment, in 1877, of the Colombo Museum, still arguably the most prominent piece of architecture in Colombo. Natural history studies flourished on the island, albeit mainly in the hands of European visitors and settlers, P. E. P. Deraniyagala being the rare exception among native Sri Lankans to make an outstanding contribution to the field.

Sri Lanka's association with foreign scientists, naturalists and conservationists continues, with recent examples including work on whales and dolphins (Hal Whitehead, Abigail Alling, Jonathan Gordon and others in the 1980s, and more recently Charles Anderson), dragonflies (for example Matjaž Bedjanič and Karen Conniff) and primates (Wolfgang Dittus and Anna Nekaris). One of the most significant recent interventions by a foreign naturalist was by Swiss national and Chairman Emeritus of the Ceylon Bird Club Thilo Hoffmann, who spearheaded a campaign to save the Sinharaja rainforest from logging in the 1970s.

Botany has had a strong scientific tradition supported by government institutions, not least the two-centuries old Royal Botanic Gardens at Peradeniya, and has witnessed projects such as the 15-volume *A Revised Handbook to the Flora of Ceylon* (M. D. Dassanayake, F. R. Fossberg and W. D. Clayton, eds, 1980–2004), which updated an earlier key work by Henry Trimen (*A Hand-book to the Flora of Ceylon*, 1893–1900). Botany was integrated into the wider ecological and biogeographical context by later botanists such as Nimal and Savithri Gunatilleke, with their long-time collaborator Peter Ashton.

In the 1980s Rohan Pethiyagoda founded the Wildlife Heritage Trust, which included notable field workers such as Kelum Manamendraarachchi, and their range of work made key contributions to discovering new species, especially among amphibians, fish, freshwater crabs and reptiles. They overturned the notion that Sri Lanka was well explored biologically, and spawned a renaissance in biodiversity exploration. A number of Sri Lankan scientists now work in subjects from land molluscs (Dinarzarde Raheem), herpetofauna (Anslem de Silva, Madhava Meegaskumbura, Ruchira Somaweera and Mendis Wickramasinghe), cetaceans (Anouk Illangakoon, Ranil Nanayakkara, Asha de Vos and Hiran Jayawardene), butterflies (Michael van der Poorten), elephants (Prithiviraj Fernando, Manori Gunawardana and Shermin de Silva) and primates (Jinie Dela), to ornithology (Ceylon Bird Club and the Field Ornithology Group of Sri Lanka), to take a small sample of workers. In the 1990s and the first decade of the 2000s, the Sri Lanka office of the IUCN, staffed by people such as Shiranee Yasaratne and Channa Bambaradeniya, proactively engaged with the private sector and also produced a raft of scientific and popular publications.

The current work was preceded by an important period in the early 1980s, which saw a home-grown conservation movement led by organizations such as March for Conservation. Part of this movement was the charismatic Sarath Kotagama, who took birdwatching to the Sinhala reading public and followed in the tradition of British wildlife popularizers such as G. M. Henry and John and Judy Banks, publishing pictorial guides to birds, mammals and butterflies.

Unfortunately, the Convention on Biological Diversity (CBD) has been seized by 'patriots' to raise the red herring of international biopiracy. Although the intentions of some of the detractors may at times be noble, their actions are counter-productive to Sri Lankan natural history. One unintended consequence of the CBD has been to create an environment that is hostile to research and stifles international engagement. A response to this has been the emergence of the 'Monetization School', led by people like myself, who have complemented or even turned away from research as the prime focus, to the socio-economic benefits of wildlife conservation. We argue that conservation is justified, and indeed vital, in wildlife-rich parts of the island on the grounds of 'ecosystem benefits' and direct translation into cash at the bank, through the creation of livelihoods from wildlife tourism.

Left: 'Nillu-hanging bushes and bamboos in the highlands of Ceylon', *an illustration executed ca February, 1882, by the German biologist and champion of Charles Darwin, Ernst Heinrich Haeckel (1834–1919). Haeckel was in Sri Lanka from November 1881 to March 1882, collecting marine invertebrates and executing dozens of watercolour landscapes of the island. In 1883 he published* A visit to Ceylon, *a colourful and atmospheric account in English of his exploration of Sri Lanka. Nillu is the local name for shrubs of the genus Strobilanthes, of which several dozen species are endemic to the highlands. The mauve flowers illustrated, however, though heavily stylized, appear to be* Coleus inflatus, *not 'nillu'.*

Species Coverage

The main focus is on animal groups (taxons in technical parlance), for which there is a wide public appetite. I do not in any way doubt the value of the ecological role performed by earthworms and bees (for example), but I have taken the view that people would rather travel to Sri Lanka to see Blue Whales and Leopards. *Wild Sri Lanka* therefore focuses on the flagship species and groups that people want to see.

I have tried to move away from a textbook style and have often written in the first person, providing extracts from my journals to give an idea of what one may actually see in the field. Where possible, the general accounts indicate the likelihood of seeing a species, and mention of species that may be recorded at a site but are difficult to see has been avoided. All too often, publications describe highly desirable animals; what they do not state is that only scientists operating camera traps are likely to see them. I have also tried to share the spirit of adventure and excitement of finding new things by describing some of the activities I have engaged in. I hope you will enjoy the chance to share in my adventures, and to learn about some of the island's remarkable wildlife.

Sri Lanka's Top Wildlife

Sri Lanka has a strong claim to be the best wildlife destination in the world. No other country has its combination of endemic biodiversity, large land mammals, marine mammals, especially the Blue Whale (*Balaenoptera musculus*) and Sperm Whale (*Physeter macrocephalus*), and diverse landscapes in such a compact area. Sri Lanka is:

- The best for big-game safaris outside Africa.
- One of the top whale-watching destinations in the world.
- The ultimate island safari.

Marine Wildlife

Best in the world

- Blue Whales. December to mid-April from Mirissa. In Trincomalee, the peak encounter rate is in March and April, but the season extends to August.
- Super-pods of Sperm Whales. Kalpitiya from December to April. Trincomalee from March to April.
- A chance to see Blue and Sperm Whales on the same sailing. Mirissa and Trincomalee, seasons as above.
- Shore-based site (Swamy Rock) for watching Blue Whales. Trincomalee, seasonal.

Other marine wildlife

- Super-pods of Spinner Dolphins (*Stenella longirostris*) off Kalpitiya. December to mid-April.
- Five species of marine turtle come ashore to nest; months vary by species.
- Snorkelling and diving. West, south coast and Kalpitiya from December to mid-April. East coast (for example Trincomalee), March to August.

Above: *The tail flukes of Sperm Whales are used in photo identification of individual animals to study their movements. The smooth, undamaged edges suggest that this could be a young animal.*

Opposite: *Blue Whales off Sri Lanka seem to fluke up on 90% of the dives compared to Blue Whales off California which fluke up only on 10% of dives.*

Left: The Elephant Gathering probably has important social implications allowing animals from related groups to renew acquaintances. It provides the opportunity for mature bulls to seek out receptive females in 'on-plain dating'.

Terrestrial Wildlife

Best in the world

- The Elephant Gathering (Minneriya and Kaudulla), the largest annually recurring concentration of wild elephants in the world. June to September, peaking in August.
- Leopard (*Panthera pardus kotiya*). Year-round in Yala and Wilpattu.
- Sloth Bear (*Melursus ursinus*). Both Yala and Wilpattu are good places to see this species, especially during the Palu (*Manilkara hexandra*) fruit season in June and July.
- The only game park (Uda Walawe National Park) where elephant sightings are guaranteed on every game drive. Year-round.
- The largest and longest studied bird wave (Sinharaja), offering the best viewing of a bird wave. Year-round.

Other wildlife

- Thirty-three endemic bird species (see page 198 for list). Year-round but rainforests drier during December to March.
- Dragonfly hot spot. More than half the species are endemic. Year-round.
- Night safaris for lorises and other nocturnal mammals. Year-round, both on private land and on public roads.
- Staggering biodiversity. Year-round. Over half the native freshwater fish are endemic. There are 245 species of butterfly, 23 of which are endemic (see page 78). Radiation of endemic tree frogs (see page 72). Endemic mammals number 21 in total (see page 200 for list).

- Reptiles and amphibians numbering 350 species. Sri Lanka is one of the best places to see large concentrations of Marsh or Mugger Crocodiles (*Crocodylus palustris*). Seasonal, in dry season (August–September).

Good to know, but hard to see

- Rusty-spotted Cat (*Prionailurus rubiginosa*), the smallest wild cat in the world. Widespread and usually nocturnal.
- Jungle Cat (*Felis chaus*). Late evenings in Uda Walawe.

Above: *The Mugger Crocodile is the second largest quadruped (four-legged) land reptile in the world. Even Leopards exercise extreme care at waterholes to avoid being dragged in.*

Opposite: *Sloth Bears are semi-specialists and have evolved long, tough claws to tear down termite hills, which are abundant in the dry lowlands.*

Wildlife Calendar

Opposite: *KBMC1 was one of the 'media-friendly' Leopards used to publicize the fact that Yala is the best place in the world to see a Leopard.*

Key

- ● Peak numbers or best months
- ◐ Other viewing months
- ○ Rare; can turn up any time
- (blank) Insufficient data. May have a good encounter rate

MARINE WILDLIFE	Jan	Feb	Mar	Apr	May	Jun	Jul	Aug	Sep	Oct	Nov	Dec
Blue Whale (Mirissa)	●	●	●	●							◐	●
Blue Whale (Trincomalee)			●	●	◐	◐	◐	◐	◐			
Sperm Whale (Kalpitiya)	○	●	●	●						○	○	○
Sperm Whale (Trincomalee)			●	●	○	○	○	○	○			
Bryde's Whale (*Balaenoptera edeni*) (Kalpitiya)	◐	◐	◐	◐						◐	◐	◐
Spinner Dolphin (Mirissa and Kalpitiya)	●	●	●	●						◐	◐	●
Spinner Dolphin (Trincomalee)			◐	◐	◐	◐	◐	◐	◐			
Snorkelling (west coast)	●	●	●	◐							◐	●
Snorkelling (east coast)				●	●	●	●	●		◐		
Pelagics: noddies, skuas and shearwaters (Kalpitiya)				●								
Marine Turtles												
Olive Ridley Turtle (*Lepidochelys olivacea*)	●	◐	◐	◐	◐	◐	◐	◐	◐	◐	●*	●
Green Turtle (*Chelonia mydas*)	◐	◐	●	●	●	●	●	◐	◐	◐	◐	◐
Leatherback Turtle (*Dermochelys coriacea*)	●	●	●	●†	●†	●†	●†	●	●	●	●	●
Loggerhead Turtle (*Caretta caretta*)	●	●	●	●	●	●	●	●	●	●	●	●
Hawksbill Turtle (*Eretmochelys imbricata*)	●	●	●	●	●	●	●	●	●	●	●	●

*Kosgoda best †Rare nesters except in Godawaya

TERRESTRIAL WILDLIFE	Jan	Feb	Mar	Apr	May	Jun	Jul	Aug	Sep	Oct	Nov	Dec
Big game and other large animals												
Leopard (Yala and Wilpattu)	●	●	●	●	●	●	●	●	●	●	●	●
Sloth Bear (Yala and Wilpattu)	◐	◐	◐	◐	●	●	●	◐	◐	◐	◐	◐
The Elephant Gathering (Minneriya and Kaudulla)						◐	◐	●	●	◐		
Elephants (Uda Walawe)	●	●	●	●	●	●	●	●	●	●	●	●
Primates (Cultural Triangle, Hakgala, etc.)	●	●	●	●	●	●	●	●	●	●	●	●
Mugger Crocodile aggregations (Yala)							●	●	●			
Large reptiles: crocodiles, Water and Land Monitors (*Varanus salvator kabaragoya* and *V. bengalensia*)	●	●	●	●	●	●	●	●	●	●	●	●
Birding												
Sinharaja bird wave	●	●	●	●	●	●	●	●	●	●	●	●
Migrant wader concentrations (e.g. Palatupana)	●	●	●								●	●
Migrants (esp. Himalyan migrants in Nuwara Eliya)	●	●	●								●	●
Other wildlife												
Dragonflies and butterflies	●	●	●	●	●	●	●	●	●	●	●	●
Swarms of 'white and yellow' butterflies in dry zone		●	●									
Flowering of introduced trees in cities						●	●					

Big-game Safaris

It is difficult to imagine that the tiny island of Sri Lanka is the next best place to the gigantic African continent for big-game safaris. There are strong and credible arguments for this.

Sri Lanka does not, of course, match Africa as a big-game safari destination. Nowhere else in the world do you see such concentrations of big game as you do in Africa. The sheer numbers are unrivalled. However, what is the next best continent or country? One of the criteria I use to determine this is the presence of five big, charismatic mammals that inspire awe and fuel the desire for big-game safaris. The African big five comprise the Lion (*Panthera leo*), Leopard (*Panthera pardus pardus*), African Elephant (*Loxodonta africana*), Black Rhinoceros (*Diceros bicornis*) and African Buffalo (*Syncerus caffer*). Many countries outside Africa and Asia struggle to find a big five.

In North America there are the three bears, the Black Bear (*Ursus americanus*), the Brown Bear (*Ursus arctos*) and Grizzly Bear subspecies (*U. arctos horribilis*), and the Polar Bear (*Ursus maritimus*). There is also the Cougar or Mountain Lion (*Puma concolor*). However, trying to see these four species, or five if you add the American Bison (*Bison bison*), on one tour is difficult and enormously expensive. South America – though it is an area of huge biodiversity – has only the Jaguar (*Panthera onca*), which is very elusive.

In Australia there are the large species of kangaroo (Macropus spp.). Many countries have huge birds – Cassowaries (Casuarius spp.), Emus (*Dromaius novaehollandiae*) and Ostriches (*Struthio camelus*) – but the animals that make it to a big list are generally mammals. People are unlikely to fly to Australia mainly to go on a safari to see kangaroos, although they do go there (and to Antarctica) for their wildlife as a whole.

In Europe there are the Brown Bear (*Ursus arctos arctos*), European Bison (*Bison bonasus*), Grey Wolf (*Canis lupus lupus*) and lynxes (*Lynx* spp.). However, these animals are relatively scarce, scattered around the continent and generally very shy of people.

In Asia, with the exception of India and Sri Lanka, large mammals are very difficult to see. In India it may be easier to go in search of Tigers (*Panthera tigris*) than it would be to find elephants, and the Leopard and Sloth Bear are elusive. Taking into account the ease of viewing or encounter rate for these three mammals, Sri Lanka ranks well ahead of India. It does not have the most charismatic land mammal of Asia, the Tiger, or the Asiatic Lion (*Panthera leo persica*), which is restricted to the Gir Forest in the state of Gujarat in India. However, Sri Lanka compensates for this with two awesome animals, the Blue Whale, the largest animal ever found on the planet and the Sperm Whale, the largest toothed whale. Mammals are relatively easy to see in Sri Lanka and the expectations of most visitors when it comes to safaris pivot around seeing mammals. When the likelihood and cost of seeing and photographing five charismatic mammals on a two-week safari is considered, Sri Lanka is by far the better destination.

The chart below shows the viewing ranking of Sri Lanka's big five mammals in comparison to the world as a whole, and specifically Asia.

SPECIES	WORLD	ASIA
Blue Whale	1	1
Sperm Whale	Top 10	1
Asian Elephant	1	1
Leopard	1	1
Sloth Bear	1	1

According to classical biogeographical theory, small islands do not have large animals. Sri Lanka contradicts this theory. This is because until relatively recently in geological terms (about 10,000 years ago), it was not a small island. The sea levels were much lower during the last glaciation and Sri Lanka was a part of the large Eurasian land mass at this time. This resulted in large land animals being on what subsequently became isolated as an island by rising sea levels. Moreover, large land animals occur on the island in significant concentrations, giving rise to spectacular wildlife-viewing events like the Elephant Gathering. In time, more people will take stock of the uniqueness of Sri Lanka – a tiny island that is a big-game safari counterpart to a vast continent.

The Big Five Mammals

A thumbnail profile of Sri Lanka's big five mammals is given opposite. Spinner Dolphins, though much loved and which many people want to see, do not make the list because they are not very large mammals, and because there are other places in the world where they can be viewed in high numbers. The buffalo is big but does not make the list because of doubts about its origins, and also because it is not an animal that people would travel specifically to Sri Lanka to see.

Big Blue	The Blue Whale, the biggest animal ever found on the planet.
Big Tooth	The Sperm Whale, the biggest toothed whale species in the world.
Big Cat	The Leopard, the biggest cat in Sri Lanka, the third biggest in Asia and the top predator in Sri Lanka. The largest of the Leopard subspecies in the world.
Big Elephant	The Asian Elephant, the biggest terrestrial mammal in Asia.
Big Bear	One of the biggest bears in tropical latitudes. The Sloth Bear may well be the largest bear in tropical latitudes, but data on Asian bears is not sufficient at the time of writing to be conclusive.

Left: *The Sloth Bear has an elongated snout and no front teeth, turning its mouth into a vacuum cleaner in order to suck in termites after it has ravaged their homes with its powerful claws.*

The Encounter Rate

Sri Lanka provides ample opportunity to see its big five mammals.

Blue Whale Many people dream of seeing a Blue Whale. During the season the strike rate for seeing the species is more than 90 per cent off Mirissa.

Sperm Whale Between Mirissa and Kalpitiya the strike rate is good if you take multiple boat trips to sea. Trincomalee is another site with good potential for seeing Sperm Whales.

Leopard Yala National Park in Sri Lanka is one of the best places in the world to see and photograph this species. I initially publicized that five game drives offered a 90 per cent chance. Leopards have now become very habituated to vehicles, and this has made it easier to see them. At present three game drives seem to offer a 95 per cent strike rate. Every year one or more sets of cubs perform for the cameras and it has now become almost too easy to photograph Leopards.

Asian Elephant This species is found in 13 countries, but it is not an easy animal to see other than in Sri Lanka. Uda Walwe National Park is the only place in the world where you are guaranteed an elephant sighting on a game drive. In addition, Sri Lanka has the spectacular Elephant Gathering, a seasonal event in the Minneriya (and Kaudulla) National Parks. On good evenings you can see 100 plus elephants from one vantage point. There are possibly two places in Africa where a greater number of elephants may congregate in times of drought, but the Gathering is the largest assembly of elephants that recurs predictably each year, albeit seasonally.

Sloth Bear Ironically, it is easier to see a Leopard in Yala than it is to see a Sloth Bear. However, there is always an individual or mother Sloth Bear with cubs in any given year that is tolerant of vehicles and provides a reasonable chance of a sighting to serious wildlife enthusiasts who undertake three to five game drives. When the Palu trees begin to bear ripe fruit in June and July, bears can be seen on almost every game drive. Wasgomuwa National Park is believed to have the highest densities of Sloth Bear in Sri Lanka. However, due to habituation, the nature of the terrain, the density of Palu trees (a factor during the fruiting season) and other factors yet to be determined, Yala is the best place for viewing the Sloth Bear (and the best place in the world for seeing one). Wilpattu National Park seems to be as good, although more data is needed to gain a picture of encounter rates.

The chart opposite provides an idea of the encounter rates and best viewing times for Sri Lanka's big five mammals.

Sri Lanka's adoption of the big five 'label' has resulted in a strong focus on its large mammals, which until 2001 had been neglected. Before this, Sri Lanka was known in wildlife circles principally as a place visited by birders. However, for serious wildlife enthusiasts, photographers and writers, Sri Lanka's riches extend well beyond the big five and birds.

Opposite: *Young Leopard cubs often hang about in trees as this is a safe place to avoid danger. The cubs could be killed by the very animals they prey on such as Wild Pig and Buffalo. Climbing trees is good practice as even hunting adults sometimes need to shinny up a tree fast when a hunt goes wrong and the hunter becomes the hunted.*

TARGET SPECIES	ENCOUNTER RATES AND VIEWING TIMES
Blue Whale	Encounter rate 90 per cent during the season from Mirissa, December to mid-April. In Trincomalee the peak encounter rate is in March and April, but the season extends to August.
Sperm Whale	Provisionally, seen on between 1 in 3 and 1 in 5 whale-watching trips from Kalpitiya during February and March. Also seen from Kalpitiya and Mirissa. More data needed.
Asian Elephant	100 per cent in Uda Walawe (year-round) and during the Gathering at Minneriya and Kaudulla (July to September).
Leopard	Year-round. Seen on 1 in 3 game drives in Yala, with periods when it is 1 in 2. In Wilpattu, 1 in 4.
Sloth Bear	Seen on between 1 and 5 game drives in Yala. Improves to 1 in 3 during fruiting of Palu in June to July. Wilpattu may have a slightly better encounter rate.

2

Habitats and the Natural Environment

The disproportionately high biodiversity of species in many faunal groups in Sri Lanka is related to several physical factors. In terms of its geological history, it has benefitted from not being a 'new' oceanic island, but one which started off with a Gondawanaland history. It was part of the Indian plate which collided with Asia with periodic land links to the Asian mainland during glacial or 'ice-age' periods. This allowed fresh immigration of species to complement its Gondwanaland stock. It benefits from two monsoons and a mountainous interior that has created distinct climatic zones.

Left: *In medieval times Sri Lanka was a high-tech weapons supplier providing high-quality steel to the Islamic world. In the 5th century AD this international arms trade funded the Sigiriya complex whose moats and ponds are a wetland refuge for dragonflies and other aquatic animals.*

Climate Zones

The topography of Sri Lanka consists of lowlands along the perimeter, which in the southern half give rise within a short distance to the central hills that rise above 2,400 m (7,875 ft) in altitude. An examination of the topography reveals that the island has three peneplains, or steps, first described by the Canadian scientist Adams (see page 35). The lowest is from 0 to 30 m (0 to 100 ft), the second rises to 480 m (1,500 ft) and the third rises to 1,800 m (6,000 ft).

Sri Lanka can be broadly divided into four regions (low-country wet zone, hill zone, low-country dry zone and intermediate zone) resulting from the interactions of rainfall and topography. Rainfall is affected by monsoonal changes that bring rain during two monsoons, the south-west monsoon (May–August) and north-east monsoon (October–January). Their precipitation is heavily influenced by the central hills. The monsoons deposit rain across the country and contribute to the demarcation of climatic regimes.

Low-country Wet Zone

The humid lowland wet zone in the south-west of the island does not show marked seasons, being fed by both the south-west and north-east monsoons. The low-country wet zone receives 200–500 cm (75–200 in) of rain from the south-west monsoon, and afternoon showers from the north-east monsoon. Humidity is high, rarely dropping below 97 per cent, while temperatures range from 27 to 31 °C (80.5 to 88 °F) over the year.

The low-country wet zone is the most densely populated area in Sri Lanka. The coast is well settled, while the interior has Coconut (*Cocos nucifera*) and rubber (*Hevea* sp.) plantations, some rice (paddy) cultivation and small industries. Remnants of rainforest and tropical moist forests exist precariously in some parts of the interior, under pressure from an expanding population. It is in these forests that many of the endemics can be found.

Hill Zone

The mountainous interior lies within the wet zone and rises to more than 2,400 m (7,875 ft). Rainfall is generally well distributed, except in Uva Province, which gets very little rainfall from June to September.

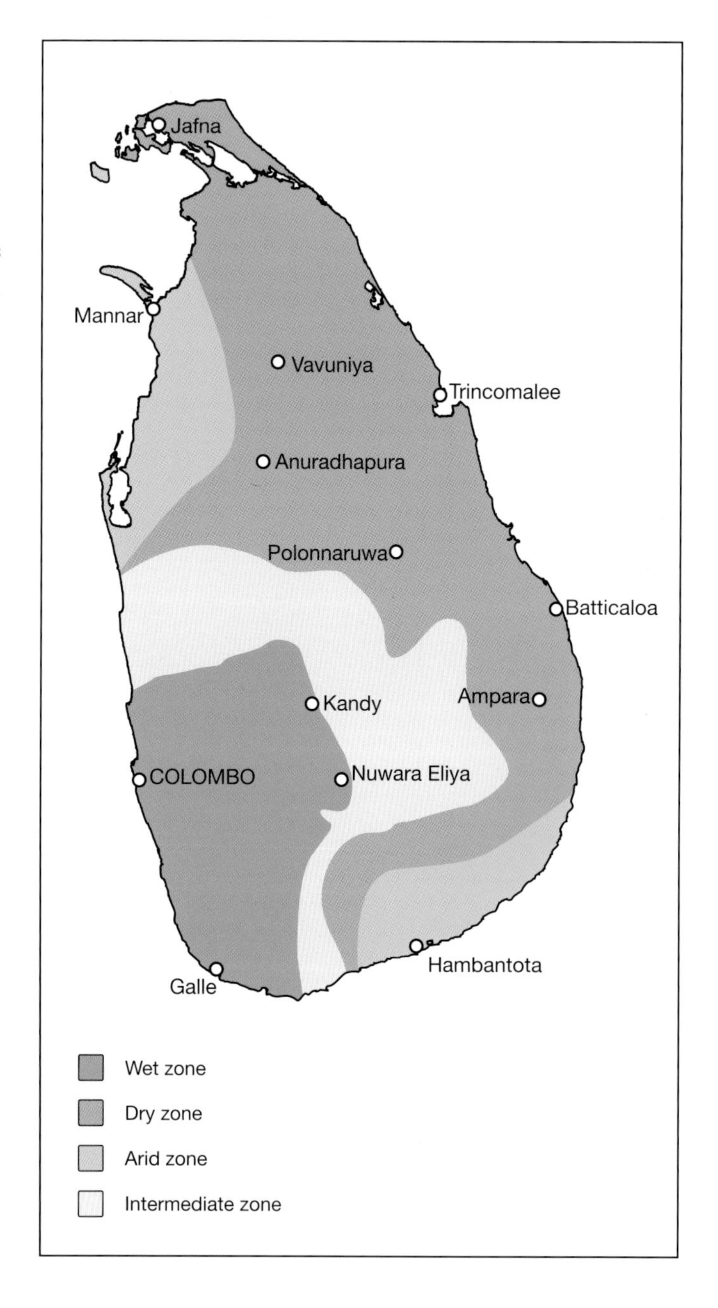

Above: *A map of Sri Lanka's climatic zones illustrates how this moderately sized island has a climatic variation more akin to that of a continent.*

Above: *The Kalpitiya Peninsula illustrates how quickly the wet zone changes into a harsh dry zone. Palm trees take the place of the luxuriant dipterocarps of the native lowland forests.*

Left: *The Annaiwilundawa wetland complex is one of the numerous man-made tanks or reservoirs, built over a time span of a thousand years, to cultivate the dry zone. Now they form important wetlands.*

Temperatures are cooler than in the lowlands and can vary from chilly in the mornings to warm by noon. In the mid-elevations, such as the area around Kandy, the temperature varies between 17 and 31 °C (62.5 and 88 °F) during the year. Temperature variations during a 24-hour cycle are, however, far less varied. The mountains are cooler, within a band of 14 to 32 °C (57 to 89.5 °F) during the year. There may be frost in the high hills in December and January, when night-time temperatures fall below zero.

The central hill zone is intensely planted with tea, but has small areas of remnant forest and open grassland.

Above: *A view onto Adam's Peak across the tea estates that have replaced the cloud forests.*

Opposite: *A view from near Haputale shows the middle and lower peneplains falling away to the sea.*

Low-country Dry Zone

The rest of the country, three-quarters of Sri Lanka's land area, consists of the dry zone of the northern, southern and eastern plains. These regions receive between 60 and 190 cm ($23\frac{1}{2}$ and $74\frac{1}{2}$ in) of rain each year, mainly from the north-east monsoon. The dry zone is further divided into the arid zones of the north-west and south-east, which receive less than 60 cm ($23\frac{1}{2}$ in) of rain as they are not in the direct path of the monsoonal rains.

The coastal plains in the Southern Province, where Yala and Bundala National Parks are located, and the North Central Province where the cultural sites are situated, are dry and hot. Much of the dry zone is under rice and other field crops, irrigated by vast man-made lakes (the 'tanks' or 'wewas'), many of which are centuries old and were built by royal decree to capture the scarce rainfall in these areas. This area was once the 'granary of the east', exporting rice as far as China and Burma, but wars and invasion, and malaria and other diseases laid waste to vast areas of the low-country dry zone. The once-bountiful rice plains were reclaimed by scrub jungle, the haunt of the Asian Elephant, Sloth Bear and Leopard. Since independence in 1948, successive governments have vigorously promoted colonization and resettlement of these areas. Sandy beaches fringe the coastline and it is always possible to find a beach that is away from the path of the prevalent monsoon.

Intermediate Zone

The intermediate zone is a transition zone between the dry and wet zones. Recent rainfall data shows that the wet zone with the highest precipitation is smaller than shown on maps of a few decades ago.

Above: *In Negombo, fibreglass-hulled boats use the wind to carry them to sea and back. The onset of the south-west monsoon rotates the fishing season from the west to the east coast.*

Right: *The Puttalam Lagoon is one of the largest and supports an inland fishery. Its mangroves are an important breeding nursery for offshore fish.*

Opposite: *The dry-zone coastal forests have species such as Maliththan (Salvadora persica) which are salt tolerant. The dry-zone flora regenerates quickly after die-backs triggered by events such as the Boxing Day tsunami of 2004.*

Temperatures

Temperatures in the wetter parts of the lowlands (including Colombo) vary between 22 and 30 °C (71 and 86 °F) during the year. In the drier parts of the lowlands they can be a few degrees higher. However, the combination of the heat and humidity in the wet-zone lowlands makes them more uncomfortable than the hotter dry zone. In the mid-hills around Kandy, for example, the temperature varies between 17 and 31 °C (62.5 and 87.5 °F) during the year. Temperature fluctuations during the day are much less and not on the scale of the annual variations mentioned. However, temperatures can vary from chilly in the mornings to warm by noon. In the mountains it is cooler, within a band of 14 and 32 °C (57 and 89.5 °F) during the year.

The period January to April is the warmest in the lowlands, but is the favoured time for tourists because it is generally the driest and also coincides with the northern winter. In the highlands around Nuwara Eliya and Horton Plains, for example, frost may be experienced in January and February.

As is evident, the pronounced climatic zones have their own seasonal variations and the climate across the country cannot be easily generalized.

The Geology

The geology of Sri Lanka is diverse, but surprisingly attracts little interest among amateurs. Commercial interests have not, however, been slow to tap Sri Lanka's mineral wealth, and from ancient times the country has been famous for its gemstone deposits.

In prehistoric times what is now Sri Lanka was a part of the ancient land mass of Gondwanaland. Towards the end of the Mesozoic era this began breaking up into the crustal plates that contained Africa, India and Australasia. Sri Lanka was a part of the Indian plate that 45 million years ago collided with the Asian plate, creating the Himalayas. Twenty million years ago, during the Miocene epoch, the seas covered the lowlands of Sri Lanka. The seas were shallow and had extensive coral reefs that are still evident in the fossil history of the limestone beds of Jaffna and the north-west coast. The limestone beds in this area have been uplifted from the sea and exhibit characteristic limestone formations like grikes, caverns and sinkholes. On the west coast around Puttalam are small areas of shales, mudstones and sandstones from the Jurassic period.

In the lowlands the estuaries and flood plains have large deposits of alluvium from the heavy soil load carried down by the rivers, especially during the monsoons. On the south and east coasts, sand dunes are common, with their orientation influenced by the direction of the monsoon winds. The continental shelf around the island varies in extent from 8 to 40 km (5 to 25 miles). At the edge of the shelf is a steep slope dissected by submarine valleys that come within a few kilometres of the coastline.

A key feature of the island's topography is its formation of three peneplains. A peneplain is a horizontal feature that is formed by erosion to create something akin to a plain. The Canadian geologist Frank Dawson Adams was the first to comment on this. He thought that the peneplains were created by erosion, with the lowest being the youngest. An alternative theory propounded by the Indian geologist Wadia is that the peneplains were created by block uplift. Consequently, the highest peneplain is the youngest and the lowest is the oldest. The Sri Lankan geologist Professor Vithanage has yet another theory. He believes that this feature is due to the nature of the underlying bedrock, causing differential erosion. Until dating is carried out, the relative ages of the peneplains will remain a matter of speculation. Ella Gap, renowned for its scenic views, is one of the best places to see the peneplains. Horton Plains National Park is on the highest peneplain.

The lowest peneplain, rising from sea level to about 30 m (100 ft) above sea level, is flat with the exception of a few rocky outcrops such as Sigiriya. Many of the outcrops have archaeological or religious structures on them. The middle peneplain rises from about 500 to

Left: Spinifex littoreus *is a member of the grass family (Poaceae) especially adapted to arid climates.*

Opposite: *Yala is fringed by many estuaries. It is one of the most diverse national parks in Asia.*

1,800 m (1,500 to 6,000 ft) in altitude. The highest peneplain has a number of rugged mountain peaks and is very uneven in profile.

The underlying geology of the island is largely composed of ancient crystalline rocks of Precambrian origin. Three complexes are recognized within these rocks. The largest is the Highland Series that runs from south-west to north-east and encompasses much of the hill country. To the west and east of this respectively are the Western and Eastern Vijayan Complexes. The Highland Series consists predominantly of metamorphosed and charnockitic sediments. (Charnockites derive their name from the amateur geologist Job Charnock, the founder of Calcutta, who discovered the rocks.) The Vijayan Complex is a varied group of gneisses and granites, which are hard crystalline rocks. In the south-west is the south-western group with a rock structure similar to that of the highland group, composed of metasediments and charnockitic gneisses together with migmatitic and granitic gneisses.

The Highland Series has a long, parallel series of folds termed the Taprobanian Fold system. In contrast, the Vijayan group does not show any regular folding. There is another distinctive band of rocks in the south-west about 5 km (3 miles) wide and 80 km (50 miles) long termed the Sinharaja Basic Zone.

Engineers constructing a dam in Maduru Oya in the 1980s were surprised to uncover an ancient dam. This suggested that ancient engineers, too, had an appreciation of the geological fundamentals in constructing large earthworks. Despite a long history of the appreciation of geology, there is much still to be learned.

Above: *Beach Halfflower (*Scaveila taccada*) is a native Sri Lankan plant that stabilizes sand dunes.*

Opposite: *Horton Plains National Park is a cloud-forest island surrounded by a sea of cultivation. Its conservation is crucial for the water cycle of the island's agriculture.*

Above: *A cutting on the Belihul Oya to Haputale Road shows a fold in the igneous rocks of the Highland Series. One theory holds that violent geological forces up-thrusted the highlands.*

Opposite: *The geologist Wadia explained the vertical topography of the island in terms of the three peneplains or tiers. From the highest, the highlands, views can be had of the middle and lower peneplains.*

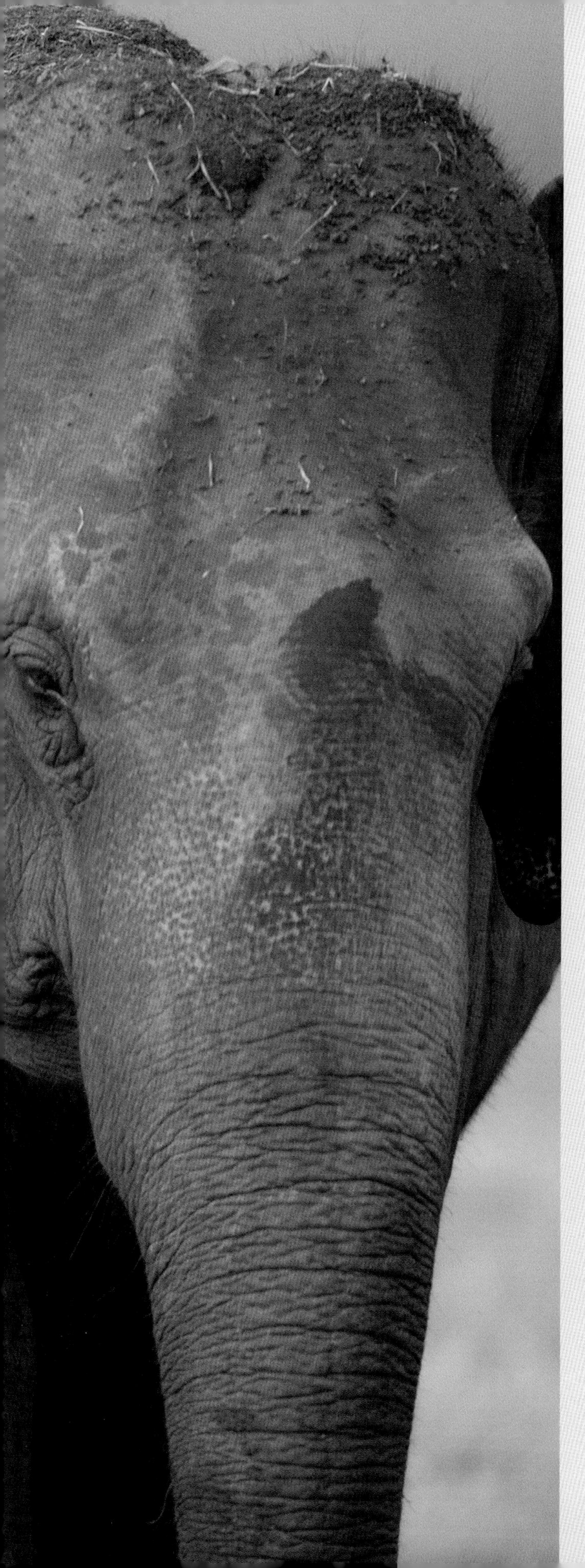

3
Fauna and Flora of Sri Lanka

A vast number of mammals both large and small, colourful birds, spectacular insects such as butterflies and dragonflies, reptiles, amphibians and plants occurs in Sri Lanka. Many species are endemic to the island, and new ones continue to be discovered.

Left: *Like humans, elephants are tactile animals. Touch is a very important part of their bonding.*

Right: Gonalabbe Meda Para Cub no. 5 (or GMC 5), a subadult male, approaches the water warily for fear of crocodiles.

Opposite: A plucky female cub attempts to drag a carcass away from a crocodile that had been feeding on it.

Leopards

I have been on Leopard safaris since the age of three, when my Uncle Dodwell de Silva used to take me to see Leopards in Yala and Wilpattu. A main plank of my efforts to popularize the Leopard was the work of the late Ravi Samarasinha, a medical doctor. He was inspired by the work of another Leopard enthusiast, the late Harith Perera, and when he was stationed at Hambantota he began to meticulously photograph and record the locations of Leopards in Block I of Yala. We would have meals together and thumb through his books, which contained a personal file of each Leopard in the park, with every encounter with an individual marked on a map with dates and times.

Samarasinha was of the view that in certain parts of Block 1, the average density was as high as one Leopard per square kilometre. He counted all individuals in this measure, including cubs and subadults. Certain observations by others support the view that such a high density is plausible in some prey-rich pockets. Photographers have had six Leopards in their field of view at the same time at dry-zone waterholes with carcasses that had drawn them in. Leopards can be drawn to both water and carcasses, so this factor should not be confused with densities. Nonetheless, the presence of so many Leopards close to each other does indicate that they occur in high densities. The researchers Andrew Kittle and Anjali Watson believe that the density of Leopards is likely to be one Leopard per three square kilometres. The actual number probably lies somewhere between one Leopard per one and three square kilometres.

This leads to the question of why Yala (and Wilpattu) is so good for Leopards. In 2002 there was a series of factors that had remained true for centuries, and now there is an added factor – habituation. The original factors fall into two broad categories: the natural underlying density and the encounter rate.

The density of a carnivore is correlated with the availability of its prey, water and denning sites, and lack of hunting by humans and predation from other hunters. Yala is a perfect habitat for carnivores because it has been modified by humans, which has maximized the population of its prey. The higher the prey numbers are in a given place, the greater the number of predators there will be. The Spotted Deer (*Cervus axis*) is the preferred prey of Leopards in Sri Lanka, and Yala has an astonishingly high mass of protein on hooves per square kilometre. If you ever spend an hour at a waterhole in Yala during the dry season, this will become obvious. Deer are abundant because Yala consists of former agricultural land that was farmed centuries ago and has subsequently reverted to thorn forest. The forest cleared for farmland has resulted in grasslands, and the park has a number of man-made lakes and waterholes. Given the abundance of foraging and water, the prey density is very high.

Due to the recent focus on Leopards, the park management has also done more to maintain water in the waterholes. Management measures include the desilting of waterholes, their expansion and even the lining of some of them with concrete bottoms to hold water. At the interventionist end of the management scale is the regular filling of waterholes with water brought in by bowsers. This reduces the mortality of deer in the dry season, resulting in an even better year-round supply of food for Leopards. Despite the many criticisms levelled at the Department of Wildlife Conservation, it has become a world leader in managing a park for Leopards. There are three key reasons for the visibility of Leopards in Yala:

- In Sri Lanka the Leopard is the top terrestrial predator. It is therefore not at risk of being hunted by other animals except for crocodiles, which will only take Leopards opportunistically when they come to drink water. In India Leopards are at risk from Tigers. In Africa they are at risk from both Lions and hyenas (Hyaenidae family). In Sri Lanka, however, they can be bold and lie about fairly fearlessly.
- The thorn-scrub terrain is open and provides better opportunities to see a Leopard than would be the case in dense forest or tall grassland.
- Habituation is an increasingly important factor in the Leopard's success in Sri Lanka. As far as I can remember, the Leopards in Yala and Wilpattu were always used to vehicles. More specifically, there were always a few individuals that were considerably more tolerant than others and provided a lot of the extended sightings, while other individuals were shy.

Due to the work of Samarasinha, from 2002 I was able to thrust specific individuals, such as Leopards JRMC1 and GMC5, into the international media, employing the coding Samarasinha used for them. In the early years it would be just one or a pair of cubs that would entertain the cameras. As Leopards attain adulthood they become increasingly nocturnal, so become less visible to visitors. However, the intense Leopard watching has ushered a change. Wildlife photographer Rukshan Jayewardene has pointed out that the park now has Leopards that are the third generation to be under the scrutiny of Leopard safaris. Their grandparents and parents have been watched intensely and have learned that they have nothing to fear from humans. The new 3G Leopard generation, as I dub it, does not have cautious parents rubbing off fear on it.

I have been in Leopard-watching log jams in Yala where people have behaved very badly. This has annoyed serious wildlife enthusiasts who prefer to enjoy a sighting without having to hear others shout across and have conversations with occupants of other vehicles. It has not, however, disturbed the Leopards, which have continued to doze on the tops of rocks. As I said before, however, visitor discipline is needed.

Those who prefer their Leopards without crowds should travel with an operator who provides for longer game drives away from the main arterial game road.

Understanding Leopard Behaviour

Leopards are easy enough to see at times. This section will help you to understand some of the behaviour you may see.

Age profiles Generally the term cub is used to describe the age period from birth to about 18 months, when offspring are totally dependent on their mother. From 18 months to about 2½ to 3 years, they are described as subadults. At this time they are beginning to fend for themselves and acquire a territory.

Eyesight Contrary to what most people think, humans have higher visual acuity than Leopards. However, Leopards have a large number of light-sensitive rods in their eyes that enable them to see in the dark, unlike us. Their eyes are six times more sensitive than ours, although colour may play a limited role in their eyes.

Jacobson's organ Leopards, in common with many animals (but not humans), have an organ at the base of the brain called the Jacobson's organ. A duct on the upper jaw is connected to nerve centres in the brain to allow for sampling of the air to take place. By smelling the urine of another Leopard, an individual can probably sex and age it and even gauge its physical condition. Thus Leopards can maintain territories by chemical warfare and avoid physical contact, which could lead to fatal injuries.

Sawing A Leopard's contact call sounds like a saw cutting through wood. The sound is usually heard when Leopards are making contact with each other. They may occasionally use it for intimidation. I have seen a Leopard sawing and pawing at the base of a tree in order to try and panic a troop of Hanuman Langurs

(*Semnopithecus priam*) in the hope that one animal would misjudge a leap and fall to the ground.

Scent marking Leopards have scent glands between the digits of their feet and on their face in the mystacial areas, and also have an anal scent gland. Opinions differ as to whether a secretion from the anal gland is mixed into the urine spray. The scent glands on their feet are probably used when they scratch or scuffle the ground. This probably is intended to leave a visual mark as well as a scent mark. Leopards often rub their faces on favourite branches and other objects, and leave scent marks when doing so. They also rub against each other and thus scent mark each other. Most often, scent marking is done by spraying urine. A male sprays urine by pointing his penis backwards and upwards. Marking the undersides of leaves may make the scent more durable as it reduces the chances of it being washed off by rain.

Sexual dimorphism This refers to a difference in size between the sexes. By the age of 15 months a male cub is the size of an adult female, and at 18 months it can be larger than its mother. Many reports of a courting pair in fact apply to a mother and her male cub, or a pair of cubs of different sexes. Even in the 21st century, these relationships are poorly understood by many of the safari drivers and guides in the national parks.

In trees Although they are the top predator, Leopards in Sri Lanka do drag kills up trees to protect them from Wild Pig and crocodiles. Cubs are also often found sleeping in trees for reasons of safety.

Flehmen This is a grimace made by animals in order to sharply draw in a breath along with the scents in the air to be sampled by the Jacobson's organ.

Territory sizes In Yala National Park the territory size of a female Leopard can be as small as 4–6 square kilometres (1½–2⅓ square miles). A male's territory size may be 4–5 times that and encompasses the territories of 4–5 females. The small territory sizes in Yala are unusual and arise because of the high density of the Leopard's preferred prey, the Spotted Deer.

Opposite: *Play fighting has a serious side. Every year subadults challenge adults and some who are not combat ready pay the ultimate price.*

Below: *Kotigala is at the intersection of multiple territories and provides an opportunity to study the dynamics of power shifts as the Leopard on the rock is constantly displaced by another.*

Left: Elephants are very protective of their young. Since the Elephant Gathering was publicized, the elephants have become habituated to vehicles and offer views of even very young babies.

Opposite: Young bulls often tussle in preparation for battle later on, but perhaps also to establish friendships for the bachelor groups that they will form when they leave the natal group.

Elephants

Sri Lankan wildlife defies conventional wisdom. Small islands are not supposed to have large animals. Someone forgot to tell this to the elephant, the largest terrestrial mammal occurring in Sri Lanka. Moreover, not only is the Asian Elephant found in Sri Lanka, but also the largest annually recurring concentration of wild elephants anywhere in the world takes place on the island (see page 50).

Understanding Elephant Social Behaviour

Family structure Studies on elephants in Sri Lanka by Dr Prithiviraj Fernando, Dr Devaka Weerakoon and Manori Gunawardene suggest that the social structure of the Asian Elephant is not as matriarch led as has been shown in studies of the African Elephant. However, as in Africa, in Sri Lanka the family units are led by adult females, with males that have attained sexual maturity leaving to form bachelor groups or, when much older, roaming as solitary bulls. In national parks such as Minneriya and Kaudulla, visitors can watch older females lead their clans to water, with the whole clan taking care to safeguard the baby elephants, which are always flanked by adults.

The basic unit of elephant family society is a mother and calf, part of a family unit. Family units form kin or bond groups that are closely related. A number of bond groups form clans, which coalesce into herds when, for example, they converge on Minneriya in a common quest for food, water, cover and mates. The smaller herds group into even larger herds, sometimes numbering more than a hundred elephants. Herds are not stable social structures and form when there are environmental pressures that bring them together. In Yala, for example, you almost never see a large herd of elephants; at most, they aggregate at the kin or bond group level.

Bachelor life When a bull elephant attains maturity he is expelled from the herd and wanders as a bachelor. Some expelled bulls form bachelor herds in the same way as Sperm Whales do. Both species have close parallels in their social lives. At the Gathering it is possible that bulls that have not seen each other for a while renew acquaintances. They can be seen tussling for dominance while calves play with each other. In Minneriya adult bulls mix freely, using their trunks to test the air for adult females that are ready for mating.

Life as a bachelor male is not easy. Size matters and elephants get continuously bigger as they get older. Hence it is the older and bigger males that have the best chances of mating with the females. A male may not get to have sex until it is in its mid-thirties. This leaves it with plenty of time to get ready for some life-or-death battles. In October 2012 I photographed two young bulls in a mock fight. I was surprised to see how one bull repeatedly tried to grasp the back leg of the other to throw it off balance, as in a judo fight. The bulls also used their prehensile trunks to grab each other's tails. Look carefully at elephants the next time you are with a herd to spot the broken tails.

The post-reproductive female A marine biologist interested in complex social structures once told me that knowledge is the currency of females. Why animals such as humans, elephants and Sperm Whales have post-reproductive females that live to great ages is one of those questions that fascinate evolutionary biologists. Perhaps it is because of the great repository of knowledge that the older females of these species have to guide their groups to areas with water and food in adverse conditions? The older females will have many related young in a group carrying their genes. Using their accumulated wisdom to look after the young may be a way of ensuring that their genes are passed on successfully to future generations.

Territories Elephants (and Sperm Whales) have a common problem in that their food is widely dispersed and optimum conditions for food availability can be subject to seasonality. Thus it may not be efficient to defend a small territory. Instead, a female-dominated family group has a large home range that can overlap considerably with the home ranges of other elephant groups, with shared areas such as the lakes in Minneriya and Kaudulla.

Musth Bull elephants periodically go through a period when they are in a heightened state of sexual tension known as musth. A sticky dark liquid oozes from a temporal gland behind the ear. Their bodies are turbo-charged with hormones. They often dribble urine on to their legs, and have a distinct odour to them. This behaviour signals to both males and females that they are in musth. A bigger bull not in musth will give way to smaller bull in musth. Bulls in musth are aggressive, and captive elephants are often not used for work during musth.

Tuskers In the African Elephant both males and females carry tusks. In the Asian Elephant only the males do. In Sri Lanka, it is estimated that only 5–6 per cent of the males carry tusks. It is suspected that this is partly because the males with tusks have been removed from the wild population by capture or hunting for ivory. In the absence of baseline data this may have to remain a conjecture. However, the question of why female Asian Elephants evolved without tusks remains open.

Infrasound Elephants communicate over long distances using infrasound that is too low pitched for humans to hear. I once saw a lone bull standing motionless with its trunk touching the ground. Other safari vehicles drove up and went away, with the occupants thinking nothing was going on. I suspected that it was engaging in infrasound communication, and sure enough another bull soon rocked up and a fight ensued.

On the soles of their feet, elephants also have layers of nerves called pacininian corpuscles, which are arranged like the layers in an onion. They help them to use seismic communication by stomping their feet. It has been speculated that they may help them to hear infrasounds generated by seismic activity. There were reports that elephants fled the Boxing Day tsunami of 26 December 2004. After interviewing park staff I concluded that there was no conclusive evidence for this. The radio-collared elephants being studied by Dr Fernando showed no response to the seismic activity either. In April 2012 I was in Yala shortly before a tsunami warning was issued following an undersea earthquake off Indonesia. Two bull elephants within 500 m (1,500 ft) of the sea showed no movement for over an hour. Similarly, the local whale-watching boats did not report any unusual activity from marine mammals, although one foreign underwater photographer claimed that there was a sudden disappearance of marine mammals. It cannot be ruled out that elephants and whales react to seismic events, which they identify as threats. However, if they do so this may be well in advance of the events, and done extremely subtly, so that we do not notice any sudden changes in behaviour.

Right: Like in a scene out of Africa, elephants roam the plains of the Minneriya Lake.

The Elephant Gathering

Every year the Gathering takes place on the receding shores of the Minneriya Lake, in the North Central Province of Sri Lanka. Lonely Planet have listed it among the top ten wildlife events in the world, and Wild Travel have included it in the list of top 100 natural events to see. I refer here to the elephants gathering at Minneriya Lake because this is where most people go to see them. However, what is written about Minneriya applies equally to the nearby Kaudulla National Park, which is another lake fringed with scrub jungle. Each of these parks has its regulars, but the elephants also move between the parks under the jurisdiction of the Department of Wildlife Conservation. They also occupy the Hurulu Nature Park managed by the Forest Department, which does not have a large lake within it, and the elephants are harder to see here given the absence of open country. During the wet season, when vehicle access to Minneriya and Kaudulla is limited because of soggy ground, the safari operators switch to Hurulu. Viewed as an 'elephant triangle', the Minneriya-Kaudulla-Hurulu complex has Hurulu in the east, Minneriya to the west and Kaudulla to the north.

As the dry season fastens its grip on the dry lowlands, leaves wither and fall in the dry monsoon forests, and waterholes evaporate into cakes of cracked and parched mud. The elephants must move on in search of food and water. They converge onto the receding shores of Minneriya Lake (a lake is known locally as a tank). Elephants are surprisingly difficult to count. In the forest they cannot be seen at all. When they are in the open they cover each other and may still be under-counted. At Minneriya further problems arise. The elephants group and regroup as an evening wears on, sometimes entering the forest and re-emerging elsewhere. On 1 October 2001 I counted 300 elephants on one visit, and on 22 September 2002 there were 250. These counts seemed modest compared with those done a few years later by park staff, who saw as many as 450 elephants on some days. In 2008 Manori Gunawardene engaged in a two-year study of elephants in the Minneriya-Kaudulla-Hurulu complex. She estimates that the maximum count at Minneriya on an evening was 260 individuals, with a mean count of 128.

The only truly accurate way to count animals is to identify unique individuals through techniques such as photographic identification. Were some of the early counts over-estimated by double counting, or has the distribution of elephants changed? We may never know in the absence of systematic scientific counts in the early 2000s. I have reasonable confidence in my estimate of October 2001 because I had counted the elephants while driving along in one direction, and had not counted them on the way back, largely eliminating the possibility of double counting.

It should also be noted that these are largely populations of elephants that live in the area throughout the year. Initially it was speculated that elephants from as far away as the jungles of Wasgomuwa and Trincomalee may have gathered here. This has not been supported by radio-collaring data. Furthermore, Gunawardene's year-round data collection, using photographic identification, concludes that the population is resident in the Minneriya-Kaudulla-Hurulu area. Nevertheless, visitors witness seasonally what is essentially a gathering of elephants.

The Gathering at Minneriya is a wonderful opportunity for both wildlife enthusiasts and casual travellers to observe the social dynamics of elephants. The Minneriya tank is an ancient man-made lake constructed by King Mahasen in the 3rd century AD. Many centuries ago these lowlands were farmed for agriculture by an ancient civilization whose mastery of hydraulics was remarkably sophisticated. Today, the ancient reservoir fills during the north-east monsoon and gradually shrinks as the dry season fastens the lowlands in a torpid grip. As the waters recede lush grassland sprouts, attracting elephants in search of food. The lake always retains some water and is surrounded by scrub jungle, which provides shade during the heat of the day. The Asian Elephant is a shade-loving animal. It is not endowed with as good an air-conditioning system as its African cousin, which has larger ears. As evening falls the elephants emerge from the scrub, coalescing into larger herds.

The Elephant Gathering in Minneriya.

The Gathering is one of the most unforgettable and fantastic events in the international wildlife calendar. However, there are threats to it. The first is from competition for land for agriculture. Gunawardene has at the time of writing observed what she believes is a reduction in body condition of some of the animals. This could be as a result of elephants losing access to areas in the Kantalai area where they foraged before – in the post-war era this area has seen an intensification in agriculture. The other threat is the lack of enforcement of responsible behaviour by visitors. A strong warden will insist that safari vehicles are parked in a line so that the elephants have easy access to water and grass, and are not harried by vehicles. As they are used to vehicles, they often mill around them of their own choosing. Many of the tourism companies, especially the larger and long-established ones, favour responsible elephant watching. All visitors have a role to play by encouraging their drivers to act responsibly. A 'back-of-the-envelope' calculation suggests that the Gathering could generate a billion rupees in room revenues alone. This is a huge amount of recurrent revenue, which can support local livelihoods. However, for it to be sustainable at the micro level, the elephant watching needs to be done responsibly, and at the macro level much larger spatial scale issues need to be resolved to ensure that elephants can range over a wide area to feed as well as to maintain the gene flow within populations.

Key Facts

When should I visit? The Gathering begins around June and peaks during the months of August and September. It starts to tail off in October with the onset of the north-east monsoon. The locals know whether the herds are gathered in Minneriya National Park, or whether the nearby Kaudulla National Park offers better viewing at a particular time. Visitors should be guided by local advice and be flexible as to which of the parks they visit.

Why is it called the Gathering? This is a seasonal viewing in the dry season of large numbers of elephants from a population that is resident in the area, which gather on the lake bed. It is not a migration of elephants.

How should I visit? Choose a reputable tour operator who can make your arrangements for accommodation, park-entry fees, safari-jeep hire, and so on. Hotels in the neighbourhood can also make arrangements for jeep safaris. Make sure your vehicle driver engages in responsible elephant watching and gives the animals plenty of space. The choice to be close to a vehicle is a decision that the elephants must make; visitors should avoid driving right up to them.

What else can I do while I am there? Minneriya, which is the focus of the Gathering, is at the centre of one of the richest areas for culture and archaeology. The magnificent ancient cities of Anuradhapura and Polonnaruwa, the rock-fortress palace of Kasyappa at Sigiriya and the Golden Rock Temple of Dambulla are all within a half day's excursion. Wildlife and culture enthusiasts may like to visit the Ritigala archaeological and forest reserve. Polonnaruwa and Sigiriya are outstanding archaeological sites that are also good for watching primates. Many of the country's finest hotels are located within half an hour to an hour's drive of Minneriya.

Sloth Bears

Sloth Bears are largely nocturnal mammals, which explains why in Wasgomuwa they are almost impossible to see despite the fact that the park is rumoured to have the highest density of Sloth Bears in the country. Fortunately, in Yala the bears are more tourist friendly and can be seen gorging themselves on ripe Palu fruit or hurrying along somewhere.

Bears are great omnivores. In the northern latitudes they are famous for alternating between berries and salmon, depending on which are in season. The Sloth Bear has taken an evolutionary gamble by heading halfway down the road to specialism. It is a semi-specialist in termites. It has lost its front teeth and has flexible protrusible lips and nostrils that can seal, so that it can hoover in termites. Its prey does not give in easily and has taken refuge inside termite hills that can be as tough as concrete. The Sloth Bear carries the tools for the job, having powerful claws for ripping down termite hills. The same powerful tools can inflict serious injury to humans who stumble across a bear, although Sloth Bears rarely eat meat. Many forest villagers have been badly mauled with bites to the head or swipes to the face. Attacks occur mostly in fields and adjacent forest, where people and bears forage for the same food. I have asked many experienced forest people what the best strategy is for dealing with a bear charge – whether to hold your ground or run. Opinion is divided.

Sloth Bears share communal dens, but are generally seen as solitary animals with the exception of mothers with cubs. Wilpattu has a strong reputation for bears, with some arguing that the chances of seeing them are better there than in Yala.

Primates

Sri Lanka offers outstanding opportunities to observe primates at close quarters. There are three species of diurnal primate, the Hanuman or Grey Langur, Purple-faced Leaf Monkey and Toque Monkey or Toque Macaque (*Macaca sinica*). The Purple-faced Leaf Monkey and Toque Monkey are endemic, with the Purple-faced having four distinct races and the Toque having three. The following are among the best sites for primates.

Above: *The Purple-faced Leaf Monkey must be one the few endemic primates to be found in a capital city.*

Top left: *The mood of a Sloth Bear is hard to read and if surprised it can inflict savage injuries on people.*

Talangama Wetland

The Talangama Wetland is a 30–45-minute drive from central Colombo. It is a reliable location in which to see the Critically Endangered western race of the Purple-faced Leaf Monkey (*Semnopithecus vetulus nestor*). It is also good for birds and dragonflies, and for observing traditional rural life. In the late 1990s a housing boom resulted in a lot of the land here being carved up into blocks and sold. The new owners took out the old trees that were the traditional boundary-line markers. As a result, much of the tree cover that the leaf monkeys need was lost. The presence of Jak (*Artocarpus heterophyllus*) trees, which bear large fruit at one time, sustained a population density that was probably higher than in a natural forest. Unfortunately the loss of habitat and the increase in dogs, with more people and a lack of understanding of the need to use monkey-proof roofing sheets rather than clay tiles, have led to the monkeys losing ground and increasing friction with people.

Hakgala Botanical Gardens

The Hakgala Botanical Gardens are a 15–20-minute drive from the highland town of Nuwara Eliya. Above them is the Hakgala Strict Nature Reserve, a refuge for rare montane plants and animals. The montane races of both the Purple-faced Leaf Monkey, known as the Bear Monkey (*Semnopithecus vetulus monticola*), and the Toque Monkey are most easily seen here. Both are used to people, the Toques at times seeming alarmingly casual. They have sharp canines and visitors should not feed them. Elsewhere, the Bear Monkey is usually very shy and crashes away at the merest hint of people. In Hakgala, however, troops often engage in play fighting and other interesting behaviour if you watch them from a comfortable distance. The Bear Monkey can also be seen on the road leading to Horton Plains National Park and within the park. Despite the huge number of visitors to Horton Plains, these monkeys still remain very shy.

Udawattakale, Kandy

The forbidden forest of the ancient Kandyan kings is on a hill behind the famous Temple of the Tooth Relic, which overlooks the Kandy Lake. The wet-zone race of the Toque Macaque, known as the Dusky Toque (*Macaca sinica aurifrons*), reigns supreme here, in large quarrelsome troops. You should not feed the macaques – doing so encourages aggression among these monkeys, which are already emboldened. I remember a visit when my eldest daughter was a little baby. The monkeys slowly descended and began to circle us in a sinister manner like a gang contemplating a child abduction. They had probably smelt food which was the target, but spooked my wife more than any elephant charge ever did.

Above: *An endemic Toque Monkey giving a threat yawn.*

Right: A Hanuman Langur with its baby shows maternal bonds with which we can identify.

Opposite top: The Ceylon Scaly Thrush has a large, dagger-like bill.

Opposite centre: The Spot-winged Thrush ventures into the open at twilight and dusk.

Opposite bottom: The once-shy Ceylon Blue Magpies in Sinharaja now inspect visitors with an apparently disapproving eye.

Sigiriya and Polonnaruwa Archaeological Reserves

The archaeological sites in the North Central Province are surprisingly rich in primates, with the dry-lowland race of the Toque Macaque (*Macaca sinica sinica*), the northern race of the Purple-faced Leaf Monkey (*Semnopithecus vetulus philbricki*) and the Hanuman Langur all occurring in troops together. The leaf monkeys are less shy than elsewhere at these heavily visited sites but, being leaf-eaters, are not likely to show an interest in your sandwiches. The Hanuman Langurs and Toque Macaques are both quite bold, and the latter will steal your food given the chance. *The Temple Troop*, a BBC production, was based on the Toques studied for several years by Dr Wolfgang Dittus. In one of the longest ongoing field studies in the world, his local field staff and volunteers continue to collect data every day. The public areas of Sigiriya and Polonnaruwa are also very good for the nocturnal Grey Slender Loris (*Loris lydekkerianus*). If you are watching lorises at night, make sure you do this responsibly and only use a weak light with a red filter on it. Do also keep an eye out for elephants, which can be dangerous.

The Rainforests of Galle

Kottawa, Hiyare and Kanneliya are rainforests that can be reached from Galle. Kottawa and Hiyare are within a half hour's drive; Kanneliya is at least one-and-a-half hours away. The southern race of the Purple-faced Leaf Monkey (*Semnopithecus vetulus vetulus*) occurs in small, very shy troops in these lowland rainforests. The nocturnal and endemic Red Slender Loris (*Loris tardigradus*) also lives here, but is hard to find. Some of the leaf monkeys have a white form that can be seen in troops with the normal colour phase of the southern race. The southern race has a lot of white on the thighs and almost looks as though it is wearing a pair of white shorts. Its tail has more white than the tails of the other races.

Birds

Islands are marvellous engines for evolutionary dynamics to work in, resulting in speciation. When it comes to birds, the theorists have got it right. Sri Lanka has 33 endemic bird species (for full list, see page 198). After a lapse of over a century since the Ceylon Whistling-thrush (*Myophonus blighi*) was described, a new species of owl, the Serendib Scops-owl (*Otus Thilohoffmanni*), was discovered in 2001. This raises the exciting possibility that other nocturnal species may be discovered. Could it be that another owl, nightjar (Caprimulgidae spp.) or rail (Rallidae spp.) exists, or even a strange nocturnal bird that fills the niche occupied by treecreepers (Certhiidae spp.), which occur in a cosmopolitan range, but are absent from Sri Lanka? There is scope to imagine all sorts of wonderful possibilities that may have been brought about by the forces of island speciation.

The true number of endemics may be far higher. Sri Lanka has many endemic subspecies. On my visits to mainland India I have been struck by the differences in vocalizations, as well as morphological differences, of some Indian birds of the same species as those found in Sri Lanka. Future taxonomic revisions may see the list of endemics grow further.

About 20 per cent of Sri Lanka is within designated national parks and reserves. At the top of the list for visiting birders is the lowland rainforest of Sinharaja (see page 60). As many as 30 of the endemic species have been recorded here, although a few, such as the Yellow-eared Bulbul (*Pycnonotus penicillatus*), are confined to the higher elevations on its eastern borders. Sinharaja is also the best place to see the Scaly Thrush (*Zoothera imbricata*). At certain times of the year the endemic Spot-winged Thrush (*Z. spiloptera*) can be easy to see – almost too easy as so many birds may come out onto the paths in the evening. The gorgeous Ceylon Blue Magpie (*Urocissa ornata*) may also oblige with good viewings; surely a top contender in the endemic glamour stakes. Over the years it has become easier to see, and a flock near the research station will visit bird tables for food.

*Right: The long, showy tail of the male Indian Peafowl (*Pavo cristatus*) is used in a dazzling display during courtship.*

Opposite top left: The Dusky-blue Flycatcher sometimes hunts from an exposed perch.

Opposite top right: The Green-billed Coucal is an endemic restricted to a few lowland forests.

Opposite below left: The Brown Fish-owl often roosts in clear view.

Opposite below right: The female Ceylon Whistling-thrush is a drab brown.

A good birding itinerary also takes in Kithulgala or Kelani Valley Forest Reserve. This reserve is extremely important as it is contiguous with the Peak Wilderness Sanctuary, which makes these the only remaining altitudinally graded rainforests in the country. Kithulgala also holds the key lowland endemics such as the Red-faced Malkoha (*Phaenicophaeus pyrrhocephalus*) and Green-billed Coucal (*Centropus chlororhynchos*). Surprisingly, the small forest reserve surrounding the forest hermitage of Bodhinagala also holds the Green-billed Coucal. It additionally offers a chance to see the endemic Ceylon Spurfowl (*Galloperdix bicalcarata*). This species is widespread in the wet zone, and is even found in small forest patches.

Horton Plains National Park in the cool highlands is another essential stop. The target species here is the Ceylon Whistling-thrush, which is best seen at dawn or evening. Very reticent by nature, it has a tendency to frustrate birders by not showing itself at times. Bafflingly, at times it may hop around the grassy edges of Arrenga Pool, in full view. The best clue to its presence is a squeaky, shrill note or double note, reminiscent of a creaking gate.

The Ceylon Wood Pigeon (*Columba torringtonii*) is an endemic that undertakes local, altitudinal migrations in search of fruiting trees. At most times of the year, Horton Plains is bound to have a few of these birds. Some of the montane endemics are easy to find. The Yellow-eared Bulbul and Ceylon Hill White-eye (*Zosterops ceylonensis*) are noisy and common. The Dusky-blue Flycatcher (*Eumyias sordida*), by contrast, is quiet. Stay beside Arrenga Pool and before long you will catch sight of one sallying after insects. Victoria Park is a small park in the heart of the busy highland town of Nuwara Eliya. It has achieved a reputation with birders as the prime site for seeing key Himalayan species that migrate to Sri Lanka. Indeed, Victoria Park may be the best place in the world to see

the Pied Ground Thrush (*Zoothera wardii*), Kashmir Flycatcher (*Ficedula subrubra*) and Indian Blue Robin (*Saxicoloides fulicata leucoptera*).

As more and more people take up birdwatching in Sri Lanka, we get a better idea of the distribution of species. Montane endemics such as the Yellow-eared Bulbul and Dusky-blue Flycatcher are now found to be locally present at some low-elevation sites.

At Hunas Falls Hotel at 1,110 m (3,642 ft), the Dusky-blue Flycatcher can be seen around the lake. A jeep ride up the tea-estate roads brings you to submontane forest, where the Yellow-eared Bulbul and Ceylon Hill White-eye can be seen. A 30-minute downhill car ride from the same hotel takes you on a sharp altitudinal drop to forest patches, which are more characteristic of a lowland forest. These forests are also good for 'owling'. On my visits to Hunas Falls Hotel, I always go to local sites in search of the Brown Fish-owl (*Ketupa zeylonensis zeylonensis*), Indian or Collared Scops-owl (*Otus bakkamoena bakkamoena*) and endemic Chestnut-backed Owlet (*Glaucidium castanonotum*). I have never returned empty-handed, at times seeing all three species in one session.

The dry lowlands have their share of interesting birds such as the Yellow-wattled Lapwing (*Vanellus malabaricus*), and Great and Eurasian Thick-knees (*Esacus recurvirostris* and *Burhinus oedicnemus indicus*). A flock of Malabar Pied Hornbills (*Anthracoceros coronatus*) is always a memorable sight. A good day's birding in Yala can yield over a hundred species during the northern winter, with many migrant species adding to the tally. Indian Pittas (*Pitta brachyura brachyura*) are abundant in some years. The roads outside the park are also good for birders, with Indian and Jerdon's Nightjars (*Caprimulgus asiaticus eidos* and *C. atripennis aequabilis*) to be seen. One early morning on one kilometre (²/₃ mile) of road I counted seven Indian Nightjars.

Six kilometres (3¹/₂ miles) from Yala National Park is the Palatupana Lewaya (salt pan), which is great for shorebirds. Northern migrants throng the edges of the salt pans. Hundreds and at times thousands of waders are present. Frame-filling views of Curlew Sandpipers (*Calidris ferruginea*), Little Stints (*Calidris minuta*), Redshanks (*Tringa totanus eurhinus*), Greenshanks (*Tringa nebularia*), Pacific Golden and Grey Plovers (*Pluvialis fulva* and *P. squatarola*), Ruffs (*Philomachus pugnax*) and ... the list goes on. Flocks of Little Terns (*Sterna albifrons sinensis*) should be examined carefully for the sight of a Saunders's Tern (*S. saundersi*). White-winged, Gull-billed, Common and Caspian Terns (*Chlidonias leucopterus, Gelochelidon nilotica nilotica, Sterna hirundo longipennis* and *S. caspia*) mingle and rest on sandbanks. About half an hour's drive away is Bundala National Park. It has elephants and jackals, but its key attraction is the thousands of shorebirds. Red-necked Phalaropes (*Phalaropus lobatus*) and Avocets (*Recurvirostra avosetta*) are scarce migrants regularly reported from here.

Even business travellers to the capital Colombo will find it easy to find time for a spot of birding between meetings. The Talangama Wetland, about 30 minutes drive from Colombo, has recorded more than a hundred bird species. One March morning, when the northern migrants were still present, I clocked 70 species – not bad for a site that is a heartbeat away from the busy metropolis. It also harbours the Critically Endangered western race of the Purple-faced Monkey. The Fishing Cat (*Prionailurus viverrina*), Common Palm Civet (*Paradoxurus hermaphroditus*), Ring-tailed Civet (*Viverricula indica*), Brown Mongoose (*Herpestes fuscus*), Crested Porcupine (*Hystrix indica*) and Black-naped Hare (*Lepus nigricollis*) emerge at night, and an Indian Scops-owl or Brown Hawk-owl (*Ninox scutulata hirsuta*) will add to the tally. Most birders fit in a session here on arrival in Sri Lanka or just before departure from the country.

A two-week birding itinerary can yield a trip list of about 235 species and almost all of the endemics. Sri Lanka has been described as a birding jewel in Asia – not without good reason.

Birding Facts at a Glance

Overview About 450 species have been recorded and the list keeps growing with the addition of more vagrants. Almost a third on the list are rare migrants or vagrants. A serious birdwatcher resident in the country will have a life list of more than 300 species.

Endemics There are 33 endemic bird species. The country is an Endemic Bird Area (EBA) and generally enjoys high endemism in its fauna and flora.

Birds to look out for Some local races are candidates for splitting from the mainland forms. These include the Blackbird (*Turdus merula kinnisii*), Ashy and Jungle Prinias (*Prinia socialis brevicauda* and *P. sylvatica vailda*), and Tawny-bellied, Dark-fronted and Yellow-billed Babblers (*Dumetia hyperythra phillipsi, Rhopocichla atriceps* and *Turdoides affinis taprobanus*).

When to go For serious birders in pursuit of the endemics, November to April is the driest in the south-west, where the rainforests are situated. This period has the added bonus of migrants. However, for general-purpose birdwatching, especially for a family holiday with elephants, Leopards and other mammals thrown in, the country is a year-round destination. An itinerary can be structured to avoid the places where the current monsoon is blowing.

Top sites Sinharaja in the lowlands and Horton Plains National Park in the mountains are not to be missed for bagging the endemics. Yala is good for dry-zone birds and essential for Leopards and elephants, and for shorebirds in nearby sites such as Bundala and Palatupana. Talangama Wetland is a top urban birding site. Mannar is excellent for seasonally large concentrations of both shorebirds and gulls from northern latitudes. For business travellers passing through Colombo, Talangama Wetland is just 30–45 minutes from the city centre and is surprisingly rich for birds and other wildlife.

Above: Yellow-billed Babblers are social breeders that spend a lot of time grooming each other.

Top: The female Jungle Prinia in breeding plumage shows a distinct supercilium.

Opposite top: Palatupana Salt Pan is one of the best sites for close views of waders and a variety of waterbirds.

Opposite bottom: The Indian Blackbird found in Sri Lanka is a potential split into an endemic.

Sinharaja Bird Wave

Tropical rainforests are well known for the evolution of mixed-species feeding flocks with coherent and stable social dynamics. A good example of these are the mixed-species flocks (bird waves) in Sinharaja, a lowland rainforest in the south-west of the island. These flocks are special for a number of reasons. They are the subject of one of the longest running field studies of bird waves in the world. Field studies on them were begun by the late P. B. Karunaratne in 1981 under a Smithsonian funded project. The continuous data collected over two decades in Sri Lanka has shown them to be the largest bird waves in the world, with an average 41 individuals in attendance. The average number of species in a bird wave is 12, although it is not unusual to encounter flocks with more than 20 species. The data collected shows that 21 species are 'regular', in the sense that they have been present in more than a quarter of the feeding flocks on which data has been collected. As many as 59 bird species have been observed to participate in feeding flocks.

On many occasions I have seen more than half-a-dozen endemic birds in a flock, including the Ceylon Hanging-parrot (*Loriculus beryllinus*), Layard's Parakeet (*Psittacula calthropae*), Green-billed Coucal, Red-faced Malkoha, Ceylon Grey Hornbill (*Ocyceros gingalensis*), Yellow-fronted Barbet (*Megalaima flavifrons*), Black-capped Bulbul (*Pycnonotus melanicterus*), Ashy-headed Laughingthrush

The male Ceylon Grey Hornbill has a mainly yellow bill.

Yellow-fronted Barbets nest in tree holes as do all barbets.

The male Layard's Parakeet has a red beak, while the female's beak is grey.

The Orange-billed Babbler is always found in a flock.

(*Garrulax cinereifrons*), Ceylon Rufous Babbler (*Turdoides rufescens*), Legge's Flowerpecker (*Dicaeum vincens*), White-faced Starling (*Sturnia albofrontata*) and Ceylon Crested Drongo (*Dicrurus lophorhinus*).

During the northern winter, migrant birds join the feeding flocks. Of these the only regular species is the Asian Paradise Flycatcher (*Terpsiphone paradisi paradisi*). The nominate subspecies seen in the wet zone is the migrant race *paradisi* and not the resident race *ceylonensis*. Over a period of three years, the adult male of the migrant race turns white. Some second-year birds have well-developed tail streamers and show no hint of white, leading to confusion with the resident race. Another migrant bird seen in the feeding flocks is the Chestnut-winged Cuckoo (*Clamator coromandus*).

The bird waves have a fascinating social structure, with the key flock constituents behaving like a super-organism with defined roles for its members. The flocks also appear to have a territory and a regular pattern of movement. At certain times the guides in Sinharaja can almost predict at what time and where the 'barrier flock' will cross the road. Even though I have not had the luxury of engaging in research, being a regular visitor to Sinharaja I have gathered a 'feel' for the home ranges of different bird waves and where their daytime resting places are located. I have also learned to hurry back towards the entrance gate to catch a crossing of the barrier flock. Quantitative data on what credible conclusions may be drawn on the social dynamics of these flocks has been gathered over two decades by Professor Sarath Kotagama of the Field Ornithology Group of Sri Lanka (FOGLS). My interest in the feeding flocks was stimulated after listening to lectures by him, the late P. B. Karunaratne and others who have done fieldwork with FOGSL.

Some species in the flocks play a pivotal role. The Ceylon Crested Drongo acts as the sentinel, responsible for security and warding off predators. It also summons the flock with a special call. The Ceylon Rufous Babbler is another nucleus species. It keeps an acoustic signature on the flock's perambulation through the forest. It contributes the largest number of individuals – at times as many as 50 – to a feeding flock. Ashy-headed Laughingthrushes, Red-faced Malkohas and Malabar Trogons (*Harpactes fasciatus fasciatus*) are other species that seem to belong to particular flocks. In fact, I have never seen Red-faced Malkohas other than in the presence of flocks. It is also rare to encounter species such as the Ceylon Crested Drongo and Ceylon Rufous Babbler without another flock species being close by.

The male Legge's Flowerpecker has blue upperparts, whereas the female has dark olive upperparts.

The Sinharaja bird waves traverse the forest like giant vacuum cleaners, devouring edible plant and animal matter in their path. The presence of so many individuals together creates competition for food. However, the disturbance created by a flock also flushes insects, which affords feeding opportunities for the birds. About half of the species observed in the feeding flocks are insectivores, with the balance almost equally being frugivores and omnivores. Insectivores and omnivores would benefit from the flushing of insects as a result of a wave of disturbance.

Another benefit for the birds in a bird wave is enhanced security. With so many birds gathered together, there are more eyes looking out. A bird wave can also mob a predator with more confidence than would a smaller number of birds. Flock members may benefit from the dilution effect, by statistically reducing their chances of being the animals to be taken by predators. On the whole, the benefits of foraging in a bird wave seem to outweigh the costs, and a stable structure seems to have evolved.

Territory-holding flocks of Dark-fronted Babblers join and leave a bird wave as it cuts through their territories. Different pairs of the Black-naped Monarch (*Hypothymis azurea ceylonensis*) may also temporarily join a flock that is passing through. The species in a bird wave even have well-defined patterns as to the order in which they make a crossing of a road or clearing. Ceylon Crested Drongos and Ceylon Rufous Babblers are the first, followed by Ashy-headed Laughingthrushes, Malabar Trogons, Red-faced Malkohas, and so on. The Lesser Yellownape (*Picus chlorolophus wellsi*) is often the last to cross.

Small mammals such as Dusky-striped, Layard's and Giant Squirrels (*Funambulus sublineatus, F. layardi* and *Ratufa macroura*) also join the bird waves. Quite often a bird wave seems to have at least one or two species of squirrel with it. The squirrels, like the Dark-fronted Babblers, have smaller territories than the foraging home range of a bird wave. Therefore different territory holders join the flocks at different stages of a flock's passage.

Many bird species join bird waves opportunistically. These include White-faced Starlings – powerful fliers that can disperse widely in search of fruiting trees. Often, the only opportunity for birders to get a good view of them is when they are foraging with a bird wave. Similarly, endemics such as the Yellow-fronted Barbet, Layard's Parakeet and Ceylon Hanging-parrot join flocks, although they are not regular members that will travel all day long with the flock.

In temperate countries bird waves occur most during the winter when food is scarce. In the tropics they are seen all year long. Given the relative richness of tropical forests, the scarcity of food may not be the determining factor for flock formation – this is probably the overall benefit of having access to food while enjoying the security of numbers.

I have even noticed birds forming into bird waves in home gardens in the busy capital of Colombo. Purple-rumped and Loten's Sunbirds (*Nectarinia zeylonica zeylonica* and *N. lotenia lotenia*), Common Tailorbirds (*Orthotomus sutorius sutorius*), Yellow-billed Babblers, White-bellied Drongos (*Dicrurus caerulescens insularis*), Red-vented Bulbuls (*Pycnonotus cafer haemorrhousus*) and Magpie-Robins (*Copsychus saularis ceylonensis*) regularly form into bird waves in Colombo's gardens. In much the same manner as forest squirrels such as Dusky-striped and Layard's Squirrels join bird waves, Palm Squirrels (*Funambulus palmarum*), which have small territories, join bird waves in their passages through home gardens. The flocking in towns and villages may be a response to predation pressures from domestic cats and House Crows (*Corvus splendens protegatus*), whose numbers have increased to high densities, and possibly to the presence of birds of prey such as the Shikra (*Accipiter badius badius*).

The 'crest' of the endemic Ceylon Crested Drongo shows individual variations, with some being more 'punk-rock' than others.

Reptiles

Sri Lanka is a great place to see reptiles, although if you are not interested in reptiles you will miss a lot of them, which may be good news for those who prefer a holiday without seeing snakes. Sri Lanka's herpetological (reptile and and amphibian) inventory presently stands at 238 species of reptile and 112 species of amphibian, totalling 350 species of 'herp'. The main focus of this section is on the reptiles.

Reptiles found in Sri Lanka fall into four groups: the snakes; the four-legged reptiles such as the agamid lizards (Agamidae), geckos (Gekkonidae) and skinks (Scincidae); turtles and tortoises, and crocodilians. The amphibians are made up of three species of Caecilian (Ichthyophiidae), the remaining 109 species being Anurans (frogs). A summary of the four reptile groups and the amphibians, with the numbers of species, is given below.

Above: *Marsh Crocodiles hunt in water but at night can be encountered travelling from one waterhole to another.*

		NO. OF SPECIES	TOTAL NO. OF SPECIES
Reptiles			
Snakes	Nine families		131
Lizards	Geckos (Gekkonidae)	42	
	Skinks (Scincidae)	31	
	Snake-eye lizards (Lacertidae)	2	
	Agamid lizards (Agamidae)	18	
	Chamaeleon (Chamaeleonidae)	1	
	Monitor lizards (Varanidae)	2	96
Turtles	Freshwater terrapins (Bataguridae and Trionychidae)	3	
	Land tortoise (Testudinidae)	1	
	Marine turtles (Cheloniidae and Dermochelyidae)	5	9
Crocodiles	Crocodylidae		2
Sub-total			**238**
Amphibians			
	Caecilians (Ichthyophiidae)	3	
	Anurans (six families)	109	
Sub-total			112
Total number of reptiles and amphibians			**350**

Crocodiles

The Marsh or Mugger Crocodile is the second largest quadruped land reptile in the world and is treated warily by all animals. Fortunately it does not turn into a man-eater, although the larger Estuarine Crocodile (*Crocodylus porosus*) can do so. Bundala National Park offers the best chance to see an Estuarine Crocodile, whereas the Marsh Crocodile can be easily seen in the dry-zone national parks. Researchers on a night count once found 300 Marsh Crocodiles in Buttuwa Wewa in Yala National Park. Their highest day-time count at 5.30 in the afternoon of the same day in August 2009 was 264. Buttuwa Wewa is one place where many visitors have spent time photographing large concentrations of crocodiles at the height of the drought. It is believed to have one of the highest seasonal concentrations in the world.

Lizards

The two lizards most likely to be seen are also the biggest, and fortunately both animals are comfortable in the presence of people. The Land Monitor can cause a stir when it shuffles past tourists sunning themselves or dining beside a pool. The animal is probably after the same things. The Water Monitor, a cousin of the Komodo Dragon (*Varanus komodoensis*), is the island's largest lizard and is common even in polluted canals in cities. However, if you see one swimming in clean water while on a mangrove boat safari, it is a more uplifting experience.

A special treat in Sri Lanka are the agamid lizards. Out of 18, no less than 15 are endemic. The Common Garden Lizard (*Calotes versicolor versicolor*) is common and widespread. Also widespread but not so common is the Green Garden Lizard (*Calotes calotes*), which is

Above: The Common Garden Lizard is a dragon lizard whose aggressive behaviour can be witnessed in urban gardens.

Above right: The Water Monitor in its natural habitat.

Right: The head of a displaying male Kangaroo Lizard turns an emerald-green.

Below: The Green Garden Lizard's white vertical stripes help to distinguish it from similar agamid or dragon lizards.

Opposite: The Land Monitor is a wary animal in its natural state, but has become comfortable with people where it is not hunted.

a subcontinental endemic confined to Sri Lanka and the Western Ghats in India. The males turn their heads into a bright scarlet and appear as though they have been pumped full of blood and will burst. In Sinharaja, this is one of the most common lizards. All of the other lizards (except for the Sand Lizard) mentioned here are endemic.

The Kangaroo Lizard (*Otocryptis wiegmanni*) is common in Sinharaja. There are periods when it seems to be everywhere. A displaying male is like a spectacular mini dinosaur from *Jurassic Park*. Its head turns an emerald-green and it expands its throat pouch (gular sac) and erects a crest (the nuchal crest). Displaying agamid lizards are so pumped up with hormones and aggression that they will allow a close approach. Bodhinagala is also a good place for the Kangaroo Lizard. What was previously thought to be one species was discovered to be two species by researchers from the Wildlife Heritage Trust (WHT).

Above: The Hump-nosed Lizard is distinctive with its bulbous nose. Despite being the largest of the agamid lizards, it frequently seems to escape attention.

Top right: The function of the horn of the male Rhino-horned Lizard has attracted the attention of evolutionary biologists since Darwin, though no conclusion has been reached.

Above right: The Rock Skink is a diurnal skink which, as its name suggests, frequents rock outcrops.

The animal found in the dry zone is the Black-spot Lizard (*Otocryptis nigristigma*). The dry-zone coastal areas are also very good for the Sand Lizard (*Sitana ponticeriana*), which erects and flickers a fan-throat that is edged in a gorgeous blue. It is found from the sand dunes of Yala in the south to the sandy beaches in the northern peninsula, where it holds territories in islands of Beach Morning Glory (*Ipomae pescaprae*) creepers on the sandy beaches. Wilpattu National Park is a good place to look for it in spots where visitors are allowed to get down.

Perhaps the most spectacular of the agamids is the Hump-nosed Lizard (*Lyriocephalus scutatus*). Kottawa in the Galle area seems to be an especially good place to see it. It is the largest of the agamids but is rarely seen, although it likes clambering onto small trees. Perhaps it is naturally rare, otherwise the sharp-eyed guides in Sinharaja would find it more often. In Horton Plains National Park, montane endemic lizards replace those in the lowlands. The Black-lipped Lizard (*Calotes nigrilabris*) is common and can be seen easily. The interesting Rhino-horned Lizard (*Ceratophora stoddartii*) is less conspicuous and needs some looking for in shaded tree trunks covered in good lichen growth. The most interesting lizard here is the Dwarf Lizard (*Cophotis ceylanica*), which has a prehensile tail. It also incubates its eggs inside its body to give birth to live young, unlike the other agamids, which lay eggs. The Leaf-nosed Lizard (*Ceratophora tennentii*) is not rare but is confined to the Knuckles Range. A stop at Corbett's Gap is likely to yield one. Some species, like Erdelen's and Karu's Lizards (*Ceratophora erdeleni* and *C. karu*), have very restricted distributions in eastern Sinharaja and are outside the reach of casual visitors.

Skinks are lizards that forage on leaf litter. Several occur in Sri Lanka; the species in the genus *Mabuya* are large and the most likely to be noticed. Common and Rock Skinks (*Mabuya carinata lankae* and *M. macularia macularia*) are the two species most likely to be seen, with the Common Skink still occurring on the outskirts of Colombo. Reptiles have greatly dwindled in cities due to road kills and predation by cats and dogs. The Common House Gecko (*Hemidactylus frenatus*) is a species that continues to thrive. It is one of more than 40 species, 16 of which were discovered between 1990 and 2012 by researchers of the Wildlife Heritage Trust.

Above: The Sri Lanka Keelback Water-snake is an endemic found in rainforests as well as suburban wetlands.

Top: The Indian or Spectacled Cobra dilates its hood as a threat.

Snakes

The decline of reptiles in cities does not mean that the highly adaptable snakes have disappeared. The Indian or Spectacled Cobra (*Naja naja*) still makes rare appearances in Colombo's gardens, where they are close to natural habitats like marshes. Indian Rat Snakes (*Ptyas mucosa*) are also common and the snake species most likely to be seen. On a safari in a national park, visitors are most likely to see a Python (*Python molurus*), as most snakes are nocturnal. A Python that is digesting prey is likely to remain stationary for a while. At the Maguruwala in Sinharaja look for a pair of endemic Sri Lanka Keelback Water-snakes (*Xenochrophis asperrimus*). A widespread forest snake seen often in Sinharaja is the Green Whip Snake (*Ahaetulla nasuta*). It is a beautiful thin, long snake that is tolerant of guides picking it up to show it to people. Obviously this should not be attempted with venomous snakes such as the Green Pit Viper (*Trimeresurus trigonocephalus*), which is also seen here regularly. A few species of hump-nosed viper (*Hypnale* spp.) are widespread, but only keen herpetologists who look for them in leaf litter are likely to see them. I once photographed one which a group of birdwatchers had walked past – I only noticed it because it moved aside to avoid being stepped on. A thick pair of shoes goes a long way to mitigate the risk of snakebite, and with my penchant to go off-trail to photograph animals, I like to wear long trousers as well – but do not let me scare anyone as snakes are surprisingly difficult to encounter.

Turtles, Terrapins and Tortoises

Five of the seven species of sea turtle come ashore in Sri Lanka to nest (see page 70). Sea bathers off Hikkaduwa may also seasonally encounter marine turtles in the shallows. Waterbodies in the national parks often contain Soft-shelled Terrapins (*Lissemys punctata punctata*). Star Tortoise (*Geochelone elegans*) populations have suffered greatly as a result of having been collected for the pet trade, but I seem to be seeing them more regularly now in protected areas.

Left: A hump-nosed viper is easily overlooked as it lies in leaf litter.

Below: With protection, Star Tortoise populations may recover.

Opposite: The Green Pit Viper is one of the most frequently encountered vipers.

Turtles and Turtle Watching

The five species of sea turtle that are found in Sri Lanka are as follows:

- The Leatherback Turtle (*Dermochelys coriacea*), the largest turtle species, with adults weighing in at a metric tonne, is rare. The wanderings of the Leatherback in search of food can take it to the cold waters of the Arctic. Its diet, which consists mainly of jellyfish, can unfortunately result in death as a result of plastic bags being mistaken for jellyfish.

- The Olive Ridley Turtle (*Lepidochelys olivacea*) is the smallest of the sea turtles visiting Sri Lanka. It nests in a number of sites on the west and south coasts, including off the highly developed coasts around Colombo, Dehiwela and Mount Lavinia. Unlike other sea turtles, it does not excavate a body pit before

Green Turtle hatchling.

Olive Ridley Turtles are sometimes encountered on whale-watching trips.

it begins to lay eggs. Off the coast of Orissa, tens of thousands of these turtles take part in mass nesting, which is termed arribadas.

- The Hawksbill Turtle (*Eretmochelys imbricata*) is threatened because its shell is prized for making jewellery and other 'tortoiseshell' items. In Sri Lanka this practice is illegal. The species has a varied diet including algae, corals and shellfish, but it predominantly eats sponges (almost to the point of exclusivity).

- The carapace that is olive or brown may look 'green' in the Green Turtle (*Chelonia mydas*), but it got its name, 'Green', from the colour of its fat. It is often found around coasts with sandy beaches. Snorkellers off Unawatuna and Hikkaduwa regularly report sightings.

- The Loggerhead Turtle (*Caretta caretta*), the rarest of the Sri Lankan sea turtles, is equipped with strong jaws and a reddish-brown carapace. Its powerful jaws are used for crushing the shells of the crustaceans and molluscs it feeds on.

Turtles come ashore to nest throughout the year, with peaks for different species in different months. The two biggest rookeries for Green Turtles (and for turtles generally) are at Rekawa on the south coast and Kosgoda on the south-west coast. At Rekawa the Department of Wildlife Conservation and the Turtle Conservation Project run responsible turtle-watching programmes. Both programmes are conducted at night when turtles come ashore to lay eggs. It is best to avoid unregulated turtle-watching sessions because they may not follow the key guidelines below. While whale watching off Mirissa, I have infrequently seen turtles.

The marine national park in Hikkaduwa is a better option for daytime encounters. Habituated turtles are fed by some boat operators. Feeding wild animals is a hotly debated topic. Marine turtles face significant threats, from pollution to entanglement in fishing nets. A greater awareness of the tourism value and conservation needs of wild turtles is good. In this context, feeding a few wild turtles is small in the spectrum of conservation issues.

In 2006 a cluster of conservation organizations collaborated with the Department of Wildlife Conservation to satellite tag Green Turtles (the most abundant turtles in Sri Lanka). It appears that females nesting in Sri Lanka could have their feeding grounds in places varying from the Lakshadweep islands and the Gulf of Mannar Biosphere Reserve, to the coast of Karnataka. They could travel more than 1,000 km (620 miles) to their feeding grounds after nesting, averaging 45 km (30 miles) a day.

Young Green Turtle clearly showing the single pair of scales immediately behind the beak.

Guidelines for turtle watching

- People patrolling the beach as lookouts should not use torches because these will deter the turtles from coming ashore.

- Visitors should not approach a turtle until it starts laying eggs. Turtles may excavate more than one nest before they start laying, so it is important that visitors approach during egg laying and not during the excavation of a nest.

- Developers of beach properties should use flaps on beach lights to reduce the light seen from the sea. This will improve visitation by nesting turtles.

Amphibians

Amphibians are largely nocturnal and found in damp places. In Sri Lanka it tends to be the specialists who go in search of them. However, even the casual visitor cannot but encounter them as they are widespread, and tree frogs often use crevices or bathrooms in houses as roosts. Sri Lanka's amphibians are noteworthy. The country has one of the highest amphibian diversities in Asia, with 90 per cent of amphibians being endemic.

A spectacular amphibian story involves the species radiation of Rhacophorid tree frogs uncovered by researchers at the Wildlife Heritage Trust. The frogs have been able to radiate into a number of endemic species by overcoming the need for water at the tadpole stage through direct development. That is to say, the tadpole stage is circumvented and out of the eggs come little frogs. Another remarkable discovery was that some species bury their eggs in mud, which improves their rate of survival.

Amphibians clearly have the potential for creating an association with a country in the same way that tree frogs have done in Costa Rica. Sri Lanka, too, has some beautiful frogs, a good example of which is Asanka's Shrub Frog (*Philautus asankai*).

Unfortunately, most frogs do not show their colours well in the dark, humid conditions they often favour, and many require night safaris to see them. At Hunas Falls Hotel, night safaris can be taken on request in the hotel's private grounds. Jetwing St Andrews Hotel also conducts daytime amphibian watching, especially for children, and about nine species are regularly seen on its trips.

Left: A male Blue Mormon, one of the larger butterflies.

Opposite: The Indian Green Frog is one of the largest frogs on the island.

Below: The Tailed Jay (Graphium agamemnon) butterfly lays eggs on trees that are mangrove associates. It can be found in the capital and suburbs, which still preserve patches of mangroves.

Butterflies

There are 245 species of butterfly in Sri Lanka. If a butterfly garden is constructed, it is possible to attract more than 50 species to a site even on the outskirts of the commercial capital Colombo. Twenty-three species are considered endemic, but quite a few of these are hard to see because so little is known about them. Around a hundred species is a realistic target on a butterfly safari of two weeks' duration if time is additionally spent looking at other things alongside butterflies.

This is one of the best sites for the Cingalese Bushbrown (*Mycalesis rama*), which needs bamboo undergrowth. The species had gone unrecorded for a long time, but following the publication of basic photographic guide booklets resulting in the popularization of butterfly watching, it is being recorded from a number of other sites. On bright sunny days the footpath will be criss-crossed by Clippers (*Parthenos sylvia cyaneus*) and Blue Mormons (*Papilio polymnestor parinda*). The Tree Nymph (*Idea iasonia*) is surprisingly absent. Look for the arboreal Red-spot Duke (*Dophla evelina evelina*). The Tawny Rajah (*Charaxes psaphon*) and Joker (*Byblia ilithyia*) are two other species to look for.

Right: The Yamfly is a 'blue' which is orange. It can still be found in suburban habitats within wooded patches.

Below left: The Common Jay is easily overlooked for the Common Bluebottle.

Below right: The Five-bar Swordtail is scarce.

Opposite: The Painted Sawtooth is uncommon. It may be confused with the similar Common Jezebel.

Morapitiya

This is a good place to see the Yamfly (*Loxura atymnus arcuata*). Two scarce species that Morapitiya and Sinharaja are good for are the Common Jay (*Graphium doson doson*) and Five-bar Swordtail (*Pathysa antiphates ceylonicus*). The Great Orange-tip (*Hebomoia glaucippe ceylonica*) may show up. The Ceylon Rose (*Pachliopta jophon*), Red Helen (*Papilio helenus mooreanus*), Common Bluebottle (*Graphium sarpedon teredon*), Blue Mormon and others in the swallowtail family (Papilionidae) are large and conspicuous species that are easy to see here and in Sinharaja.

Sinharaja

Together with Kithulgala, Sinharaja is one of the best locations for the Blue Oakleaf (*Kallima philarchus*). On the main access trail near the 'barrier' ticket checkpoint is a reliable place for the Brown King Crow (*Euploea klugii sinhala*). This area always turns up a few Tree Nymphs, which seem to hang in the air like some tissue paper with Chinese symbols caught in an updraft. Near the research station is the best site in the country for the Aberrant Oakblue (*Arhopala abseus mackwoodi*), which until recently had not been recorded for decades. Look out for the Painted Sawtooth (*Prioneris sita*), which is easily overlooked for the widespread Common Jezebel (*Delias eucharis*). Damp patches of soil are good for species of lineblue (Lycaenidae spp.) here as well as in Morapitiya. At the latter I have had them alighting on my hands to sip on my perspiration. They 'mudsip' or 'puddle' to absorb essential minerals and nutrients.

The former logging road that is the main walking trail in Sinharaja is very good for seeing some of the swallowtail species. The Red Helen, Ceylon Rose and Blue Mormon patrol along the road quite often. The Gaudy Baron (*Euthalia lubentina psittacus*) is a very beautiful, widespread butterfly that is rare here. The Redspot Duke in the same family is not rare, but may be overlooked because it is arboreal. The scarce Five-bar Swordtail is another species that is easily overlooked – it may look like one of the abundant whites and yellows as it zooms past.

Talangama

Talangama is excellent for getting to grips with many of the common butterfly species, such as the Common Grass Yellow (*Eurema hecabe simulata*), and Common and Mottled Emigrants (*Catopsilia pomona* and *C. pyranthe minna*) in the whites and sulphurs, or pierids. Among the nymphalids, common species that can be seen include the Grey Pansy (*Junonia atlites*) and Common Sailor (*Neptis hylas varmona*). Butterfly species in the blues family are difficult to identify because of the similarities between some species. Talangama is a good place to start with some of the most common species such as Common and Dark Ceruleans (*Jamides celeno tissama* and *J. bochus bochus*), Pea Blue (*Lampides boeticus*), Blue Banded and Common Pierrots (*Discolampa ethion* and *Castalius rosimon*), Indian Cupid (*Everes lacturnus*) and Tiny Grass Blue (*Zizula hylax hylax*). Members of the tiger family include the Common Crow, as well as the Blue and Glassy Tigers (*Tirumala limniace leopardus* and *Parantica aglea aglea*).

The following brief extracts from my field journal illustrate how good Talangama is as an urban nature site in which to develop fieldcraft as a naturalist.

Journal Excerpts

20 January

In the One Acre reserve we saw Dark and Common Ceruleans. A Blue Tiger was nectaring on the invasive *Lantana camara*. A Glassy Tiger had its hair pencils out and was patrolling a stretch of road, wafting pheromones. It perched with its hair pencils out like the rounded brushes used for cleaning camera lenses. I was able to take a series of record shots.

3 October

Several butterflies were in evidence. A Dark Cerulean flashed through with its glossy metallic-blue wings shining against the shady undergrowth. It settled and allowed all of us a close approach. A Banded Blue Pierrot flitted through quickly. A lineblue allowed me to photograph it well. The most common butterflies, like the White Four-ring (*Ypthima ceylonica*) and Common Grass Yellow, were present, as well as the Indian Cupid. A Tiny Grass Blue stayed long enough on a legume to be photographed. A Common Pierrot (*Castalius rosimon*) was photographed laying eggs on a vine growing on a mesh fence.

Horton Plains

The key target species here is the endemic Ceylon Treebrown (*Lethe daretis*). It is easiest to see where there are thickets of the endemic Bramble (*Rubus leucocarpus*). It perches at around head height and can be overlooked. The Painted Lady (*Vanessa cardui*) is a scarce butterfly in Sri Lanka, but it may be seen here. The seeps around water will usually contain the Hedge Hopper (*Baracus vittatus vittatus*) and common Pea Blue. Bluebottles and Peacock Pansies (*Junonia almana almana*) are other widespread butterflies that occur here. The endemic Ceylon Tiger (*Parantica taprobana*) is common here, and Horton Plains is also one of the best sites for the Indian Fritillary (*Argynnis hyperbius taprobana*). The Indian Admiral (*Vanessa indica nubicola*) may be seen, but it is considerably easier to observe it on ornamental flowers in home gardens.

Right: *The Painted Lady is surprisingly scarce. It remains to be established whether some of the individuals seen in Sri Lanka are migrants.*

One of the most intriguing butterflies is Green's Silverline Lineblue (*Spindasis greeni*), described to science in 1896. There had been no records of it since the first specimen was collected, and some subsequent authors of butterfly books had it removed from the Sri Lankan list because they thought that the original description of the species had been based on a variation of another lineblue species. On 13 March 2008, naturalist Nadeera Weerasinghe photographed a female 'blue' laying eggs near World's End and sent me the pictures. Unable to identify it from the literature I had, I passed it on to lepidopterist Michael van der Poorten, who realized it was the long-lost endemic Green's Silverline.

Yala National Park

Yala is especially good for seeing large swarms of mud-sipping whites and yellows, especially after the north-east monsoon. One of the specialties in the arid zone is the Small Salmon Arab (*Colotis amata*) which, unlike other butterflies, can be seen on the wing even during the hottest part of the day. There are seasonal swarms of tiger butterflies, which often collect around the herb Balu Nakuta (*Stachytarpheta indica*). Dark Blue, Blue and Common Tigers are frequently seen clustered together.

Top: *The Small Salmon Arab is active at the hottest time of day.*

Centre: *The Blue Tiger tastes bad to predators. All species of tiger butterfly have a common wing pattern to reinforce the message that they taste bad. This is known as Müllerian mimicry.*

Bottom: *The Indian Fritillary is best seen in the highlands.*

Sri Lanka's Endemic Butterflies

A total of 245 butterfly species has been recorded in Sri Lanka. One of them, the Orange Migrant (*Catopsilia scylla*) is likely to be an accidental introduction. Harish Gaonkar of the British Museum of Natural History is currently working on a taxonomic revision of the butterflies of the Oriental region. He is of the view that the following 23 species are endemic to Sri Lanka.

Ceylon Tiger (*Parantica taprobana*)
Ceylon Tree Nymph (*Idea iasonia*)
Ceylon Palmfly (*Elymnias singala*)
Ceylon Treebrown (*Lethe daretis*)
Ceylon Forester (*Lethe dynaste*)
Cingalese Bushbrown (*Mycalesis rama*)
Jewel Four-ring (*Ypthima singala*)
Blue Oakleaf (*Kallima philarchus*)
Woodhouse's Four Lineblue (*Nacaduba ollyetti*)
Pale Ceylon Lineblue (*Nacaduba sinhala*)
Ceylon Cerulean (*Jamides coruscans*)
Milky Cerulean (*Jamides lacteata*)
Ceylon Hedge Blue (*Udara lanka*)
Clouded Silverline (*Spindasis nubilis*)
Green's Silverline (*Spindasis greeni*)
Ormiston's Oakblue (*Arhopala ormistoni*)
Ceylon Royal (*Tajuria arida*)
Ceylon Lesser Albatross (*Appias galene*)
One-spot Grass Yellow (*Eurema ormistoni*)
Ceylon Rose (*Pachliopta jophon*)
Common Birdwing (*Troides darsius*)
Black Flat (*Celaenorrhinus spilothyrus*)
Decorated Ace (*Thoressa decoratea*)

The Ceylon or Common Birdwing female is one of the two largest butterflies in Sri Lanka.

The Ceylon Treebrown is often seen on bramble.

Gaonkar recognizes the following 19 species as endemic to the Western Ghats and Sri Lanka.

Long-brand Bushbrown (*Mycalesis visala subdita*)
Glad-eye Bushbrown (*Nissanga patnia junonia*)
White Four-ring (*Ypthima ceylonica*)
Baronet (*Symphaedra nais*)
Tawny Rajah (*Charaxes psaphon*)
Striped Pierrot (*Tarucus nara*)
Ceylon Silverline (*Spindasis ictis ceylanica*)
Redspot (*Zesius chrysomallus*)
Monkey-puzzle (*Rathinda amor*)
Common Jezebel (*Delias eucharis*)
Striped Albatross (*Appias libythea libythea*)
White Orange-tip (*Ixias marianne*)
Little Orange-tip (*Colotis etrida limbatus*)
Blue Mormon (*Papilio polymnestor parinda*)
Common Banded Peacock (*Papilio crino*)
Crimson Rose (*Pachliopta hector*)
Scarce Shot Silverline (*Spindasis elima*)
Spotted Small Flat (*Sarangesa purendra*)
Chestnut Angle (*Odontoptilum ransonnettii*)

The Ceylon Tree Nymph is more commonly seen fluttering overhead, than perched.

Dragonflies

At the time of writing at least 124 species of dragonfly and damselfly have been identified in Sri Lanka, with just over half the species being endemic. The order Odonata comprises a suborder of the dragonflies (the Anisoptera) and another comprising the damselflies (the Zygoptera). The latter hold their wings closed along the length of their bodies. Dragonflies hold their wings open and perpendicular to their bodies. The specialists refer to them collectively as odonates, while I loosely mention dragonflies when referring to dragonflies and damselflies collectively.

The life cycle of a dragonfly can be described as being a transformation from a submarine to a helicopter. In the larval stage a dragonfly is a voracious predator that lives underwater and uses gills that protrude from the rear end of its body to breathe. On emergence from the water, it unfolds its wings to become a perfectly designed hunter. In butterflies, the larva (the caterpillar) undergoes metamorphosis through an intermediate stage when it pupates. This stage is skipped in dragonflies, and when the larva hauls itself out of the water and splits its skin, a complete adult emerges from inside. The newly hatched adult needs time for its wings to strengthen. This teneral stage may take up to a week and the wings have a glossy sheen during this time.

Endemism is high in some of the Sri Lankan Odonata families. All 20 species presently described in the forest damsels (Platystictidae) are endemic. Sri Lanka has a radiation of species in the forest damsels that is not seen on the Asian mainland. In the clubtails (Gomphidae) 13 of the 14 presently described species are endemic.

Much still remains to be learned about Sri Lanka's dragonfly fauna, with new species yet waiting to be discovered by science. Little is known even about the most common species. Some species described to science have not been seen since their first discovery. As I was finishing the manuscript for this book I heard about an exciting rediscovery. The Emerald Sri Lanka Spreadwing (*Sinhalestes orientalis*) had not been recorded for 150 years since it was reported from Sri Lanka in 1859 by H. A. Hagen, having been collected by J. Nietner. Recent searches in the original location, Rambodde, failed to uncover it. Matjaž Bedjanič, working through a small grant from the Rufford Foundation, located it in a forested stream on the Balangoda-Dickoya road. It is a large damselfly that he described excitedly as a 'magnificent beast' in an email to me.

Talangama Wetland

This is a good model site not only for the lowland wet zone in open wetlands, but also for the open wetlands in the dry zone. About 37 species have been recorded at the wetland, and it is an excellent site for observing a fair number of species in a short time. Five endemics have been recorded here. Three are regularly found: Adam's Gem (*Libellago adami*), the Stripe-headed Threadtail (*Prodasineura sita*) and the Orange-faced Sprite (*Pseudagrion rubriceps ceylonicum*). Adam's Gem is found perched low, close to fast-flowing water. Look for it in the drainage ditches. The Orange-faced Sprite

Left: *Talangama Wetland is a vital urban wildlife reserve and an important asset for a capital city.*

Opposite: *Juvenile Black Velvet-wings show yellow on the thorax and abdomen.*

can be found in shaded ditches and the Stripe-headed Threadtail occurs close to densely shaded vegetation. A fourth endemic, the Sri Lanka Forktail (*Macrogomphus lankanensis*), is also found here but is very rare. Another, less rare endemic is the Transvestite Clubtail (*Cyclogomphus gynostylus*), in the same family as the Sri Lanka Forktail. It can be found in canals with heavy vegetation.

The diminutive Wandering Wisp (*Agriocnemis pygmaea pygmaea*) occurs in short-cropped grass. Often found perching on the leaf litter are the Asian Pintail (*Acisoma panorpoides panorpoides*) and Blue Percher (*Diplacodes trivialis*). Yellow and Painted Waxtails (*Ceriagrion coromandelianum* and *C. cerinorubellum*) are seen on hedgerow vegetation. The Pruinosed Bloodtail (*Lathrecista asiatica asiatica*) prefers densely shaded thickets. Often found low on bushes is the Elusive Adjutant (*Aethriamanta brevipennis brevipennis*). I photographed it at Hunas Falls, which stopped Matjaž Bedjanič from removing it from the Sri Lankan list. He had thought it was an erroneous record because the species had not been recorded for more than a hundred years. It has subsequently been found to be common. One of the most common dragonflies in the wet zone, found on hedgerows and tall grass, is the Pied Parasol (*Neurothemis tullia tullia*). Another seasonally abundant species in the dry zone but also found in smaller numbers in the wet zone, preferring to perch over water, is the Asian Groundling (*Brachythemis contaminata*).

Wandering Gliders (*Pantala flavescens*) can be conspicuous when they are catching the thermals on their wings, which are patterned with patches of iridescent gold. Some of the Wandering Gliders seen here could be migrants. They participate in a multi-generational migration between India and Africa, with the Maldives serving as an intermediate stage for another generation.

Several species of red dragonfly also show themselves well, often sunning themselves beside the water or actively hawking at the water's edge. These include the Scarlet Basker (*Urothemis signata signata*), Spine-tufted and Pink Skimmers (*Orthetrum chrysis* and *O. pruinosum neglectum*), and Oriental Scarlet (*Crocothemis servilia servilia*).

One of the most charismatic species is the Blue-eyed Pondcruiser (*Epophthalmia vittata cyanocephala*), a large dragonfly that cruises over the water at great speed and disappears rapidly from view. It can perch high, hanging on vegetation above the eye level of observers and thus escaping detection. Equally charismatic, but more common and perching on waterside vegetation in the open, is the black-and-yellow Rapacious Flangetail (*Ictinogomphus rapax*), the most common of the dragonfly group known as clubtails (Gomphidae).

Two enigmatic species usually seen at dusk are the Dingy Duskflyer (*Zyxomma petiolatum*) and Foggy-winged Twister (*Tholymis tillarga*). The latter has a pale, mist-like patch on its wings and weaves a figure-of-eight pattern in flight that gives it the name 'twister'. I have seen it during hot afternoons as well, but this is a rare occurrence. It is unusual for these two species to be active at dusk, because most dragonflies are active when the day is at its warmest.

Several species of dragonfly expose themselves prominently in the open. The Blue Sprite (*Pseudagrion microcephalum*), which may be confused with the rare Malay Lillysquatter (*Paracercion malayanum*), is often found on lily pads. Other species found here include the Sombre Lieutenant (*Brachydiplax sobrina*). The females of many of the dragonflies are secretive, only coming to open water to mate. They are more likely to be seen in dense vegetation away from the water. Female dragonflies are often very different from the males, sometimes being more stripey and coloured with greens and yellows. In the Marsh Dancer (*Onychargia atrocyana*) both the male and female occur away from water, perched on low bushes and seemingly controlling a territory.

The Indian Rockdweller (*Bradinopyga geminata*) is cryptically camouflaged for rocky habitats. In Talangama and central Colombo this species occupies ponds that are lined with black rocks (usually granite) or concrete.

One of the most common roadside dragonflies in the lowlands is the Green Skimmer (*Orthetrum sabina sabina*). It is probably the largest of the skimmers (Libellulidae) and is distinctive in green and black. It is very aggressive and I have occasionally seen it eating other dragonflies. The Variegated Flutterer (*Rhyothemis variegata variegata*) is another common lowland species; sometimes a small flock can be seen in the air. It seems quite tolerant of pollution, and you can see it on canals with heavily polluted water in city centres.

Opposite left: The Blue-eyed Pondcruiser 'hangs' when perched, a characteristic of the 'goldenrings'.

Opposite right: A male Oriental Scarlet illustrates the sexual dimorphism common in dragonflies. The female is a less noticeable olivaceous brown.

Right: The Dancing Dropwing is widespread in the lowlands.

Below: The Shining Gossamerwing is common atop rocks in fast-flowing streams in the wet zone.

Bottom: The female Variegated Flutterer has clear wing tips.

Sigiriya Moat

Black-tipped (*Diplacodes nebulosa*) and Blue Perchers can be seen on the short-cropped grass as well as the reeds on some of the small ponds. Many of the skimmers are found here. The Dancing Dropwing (*Trithemis pallidinervis*) can be seen on waist-height vegetation. One of the star attractions here is the Fiery Emperor (*Anax immaculifrons*). I have found it patrolling a stretch of jungle road that was not in sight of water. It is a magnificent animal to watch as it dominates the air space. The 'reds', also common in the wet lowlands, can dominate the water's edge. They include the robustly built Scarlet Basker and more lightly built Oriental Scarlet.

Sinharaja Rainforest

The Shining Gossamerwing (*Euphaea splendens*) is one of the most characteristic species of rocky streams in the rainforests of the lowlands and mid-elevations. It is a seemingly nondescript blackish damselfly which, when taking wing, flashes a shining emerald patch. This is the dragonfly that is most likely to be noticed by people who are not dragonfly watchers.

The Oriental Greenwing (*Neurobasis chinensis chinensis*) is found in the vegetation bordering shaded streams. Occurring in similar habitat are the endemic Black-tipped Flashwing (*Vestalis apicalis nigrescens*) and endemic Red-striped Threadtail (*Elattoneura tenax*). The stream feeding the Maguruwala is a good location for these three species. Also at this location, at times perched at waist height on dead branches, may be the endemic Yerbury's Elf (*Tetrathemis yerburii*). The road close to Maguruwala contains one of the most reliable sites for the Vermillion Forester (*Lyriothemis defonsekai*), described to science as recently as 2009 by Nancy van der Poorten. I gather it was first photographed by birder Amila Salgado. It has probably been beside the former logging road for decades, overlooked by birders because dragonflies only began to be popularized in the 2000s. The Maguruwala may also occasionally have a Rivulet Tiger (*Gomphidia pearsoni*) showing up. This endemic, dressed in black and yellow, can be overlooked for the common Rapacious Flangetail.

The disturbed areas outside the forest are good places to see the Spine-tufted Skimmer, which looks similar to the widespread Pink Skimmer, but the former has a brown thorax. Marsh and Asian Skimmers (*Orthetrum glaucum*) are both found in the open areas outside the forest or in the disturbed open areas within the reserve. The males are very similar, with those of Marsh Skimmers having clear wing bases. The Sapphire Flutterer (*Rhyothemis triangularis*) can be seen in paddy fields and disturbed areas. Despite its gorgeous blue colouration, in flight it looks like a dark dragonfly with wings of half length.

The Indigo Dropwing (*Trithemis festiva*) favours forested streams that open out at a road crossing with dark rocks to perch on. It is also tolerant of disturbed areas. The stream near the Forest Department's accommodation can yield the Sri Lanka Cascader (*Zygonyx iris ceylonicum*) and Wall's Grappletail (*Heliogomphus walli*).

Bodhinagala and Kithulgala

Many of the species described for Sinharaja can also be found here, but both of these sites seem particularly good for turning up forestdamsels. Twenty species are found in Sri Lanka, in the genera *Drepanosticta* and *Platysticta*. Remarkably, all of them are endemic. Bodhinagala has a few streams crossing the road that leads to a hermitage on the forested hill. The Dark-glitttering Threadtail (*Elattoneura centralis*) is guaranteed on these streams. In the gloom the Dark Forestdamsel (*Platysticta apicalis*) seems to have a glowing blue tip to its tail. Separating the Forestdamsels is a little tricky and one needs to look at the pronotum – the section between the head and the thorax.

Horton Plains National Park

Horton Plains is the best location for seeing the Triangle Skimmer (*Orthetrum triangulare triangulare*). Look for it in the large pond beside the main entrance gate, as well as at the other smaller ponds where the road passes on the way to the visitor centre at Farr Inn. Two other species seen here easily (but just as easily in any highland wetlands, including in Nuwara Eliya town) are the endemic Mountain Reedling (*Indolestes gracilis gracilis*) and Red-veined Darter (*Sympetrum fonscolombii*). The Mountain Reedling is one of the spreadwing damselflies. Spreadwings, unlike other damselfies, keep their wings spread open when they are perched. The Mountain Reedling is the only spreadwing that does not keep its wings spread. The Red-veined Darter is not an endemic and has a wide global distribution in temperate countries, but in Sri Lanka it is confined to the highlands. The female is very strikingly coloured and is easy to see and photograph, unlike many female dragonflies, which do not show themselves. The dragonfly list for Horton Plains is still sparse because not many people watch dragonflies. I hope that montane endemics new to science will turn up here.

Above: The Red-veined Darter is one of the most noticeable dragonflies in the highlands.

Top: The female Dark-glittering Threadtail with its pale stripes looks very different from the dark glossy male.

Opposite: The Sapphire Flutterer in flight looks like a small dark dragonfly as the clear wing tips become invisible.

Butterfly and Dragonfly Watching in Morapitiya Rainforest

6 June

The main focus on this visit with naturalist guides Hetti and Jayaweera was on butterflies and dragonflies. Before we reached the tea estate, we stopped to photograph a male Indigo Dropwing on top of a rock beside a small rivulet that ran across the road. He suddenly took off and intercepted a female. She was very different in colour from him – she had a couple of stripes on the thorax and was generally a mix of greens and browns. It was hard to get a good look at her as the male that intercepted her mated with her immediately. The mating sequence took only a few seconds. She then began to rapidly oviposit (lay eggs) in the water. I asked Hetti and Jayaweera to keep an eye on the female as I had not seen one of this species before. After laying her eggs she disappeared.

I have noticed that in the dragonfly species in which males guard territories, the males are conspicuously coloured and show themselves clearly. The females, on the other hand, are often nondescript and clothed in colours that allow them to merge into the vegetation. While the female was laying the eggs, the male engaged in 'mate guarding'. This is a very serious affair for dragonflies, as a subsequent male may mate with the female and render the first mating void. Male dragonflies have specially designed penises that are grooved to remove Sperm from a previous mating.

We had more luck with photographing a female at a larger stream. I peeped over the edge and found a female Black-tipped Flashwing (*Vestalis apicalis*) perched on the waterside vegetation. A while later I also found a male and another female, which was ovipositing into submerged vegetation by placing her ovipositor on a submerged twig. While I was working my way towards the first female, sharp-eyed Hetti drew attention to two male Green's Gems (*Libellago greeni*), which were hovering centimetres above the water and engaged in a fierce territorial duel. They looked like two tiny Red Arrows engaged in aerial manoeuvres. One disengaged and went after the prize; a drably coloured female. The male clasped the female firmly and mated in less than a minute. He also seemed to perform a ritual of standing facing away from the female and raising his abdomen. The male then stayed next to the female, 'mate guarding' her, while she laid eggs on the twig on which they were perched. I suspect she was sticking the eggs to it.

***Left:** The Angled Pierrot has geometric, right-angled black shapes on its wings like a teaching aid for children.*

***Opposite top:** The Common Nawab frequents the tree tops and is seen only rarely when it descends to mud sip.*

***Opposite below:** A female Black-tipped Flashwing shows the iridescence which gives the species its name. The females lack the black wing tips of the male.*

We explored an area of paddy fields turning into marsh, where we saw common species such as the Spine-tufted Skimmer (*Orthetrum chrysis*), Pied Parasol and diminutive Wandering Wisp (*Agriocnemis pygmaea*).

We also did very well with the butterflies. A few Common Jays (*Graphium doson*) and a Bluebottle were on the road. While pausing to photograph them we were treated to a Great Orange-tip (*Hebomia glaucippe*), which settled on the ground briefly several times. The camouflage on its under-wing is so good that if you look away it may be hard to relocate it. A male Cruiser (*Vindula erota*) alighted briefly on the road. A Common Nawab (*Polyura athamas*) on the road was flushed as we drove. Several Ceylon Roses (*Pachliopta jophon*) flew without taking a break. A patch with a species of *Strobilanthes* yielded a Yamfly (*Loxura atymnus*). Several other species of blue were also present.

Without even trying we encountered a mixed feeding flock of birds. The star birds were a pair of Green-billed Coucals. Others in the flock included the Lesser Yellownape, Ceylon Rufous Babbler, Greater Flameback, Black-naped Monarch and Malabar Trogon. We did not see Red-faced

Malkohas in this flock, but we saw them later with another flock when we stopped to photograph some Angled Pierrot (*Caleta decidia*) butterflies.

The stopover at Morapitiya had taken us nearly the whole day and we left for Martin's at Sinharaja at around 4.30, having had a marvellous time enjoying the birds, butterflies and dragonflies of Morapitiya.

Trees

The dry zone is a good place to get to grips with the confusingly high number of native tropical trees. Being able to recognize a dozen important species in the dry-zone national parks makes you feel like an experienced botanist on a game drive. Each soil type defines which species of plant is the climax species if vegetative succession was allowed to progress naturally. The Palu is the climax species in the soils of much of Sri Lanka's dry zone. In June and July it bears yellow berries that are much loved by the Sloth Bear, which becomes very easy to see at this time – in fact, gorging on the berries leaves the bears in an alcoholic stupor. The deeply corrugated trunk of the tree gives it a lot of character. The rough bark also makes it a favourite rubbing post for animals including elephants. For lying on Leopards favour mainly Palu or Kohomba (*Azadirachta indica*) trees. I think this is because both trees are abundant, large, have a wide canopy providing shade and are free of thorns. The Kohomba is deeply entrenched in the ethnobotany of the Indian subcontinent. Its leaves have antiseptic values. They also retard the development of arthropod eggs – I have tried keeping a bundle of the leaves on my bookshelves in order to ward off Silverfish (*Lepisma saccharina*).

Opposite: *A Kohomba tree in high winds.*

Below: *The ripe yellow berries of the Palu Tree are a magnet for Sloth Bears, which gorge themselves on the fruit.*

The Maliththan is adapted to saline soils and is common throughout the coastal areas of Yala National Park. It is believed to be the Mustard Tree referred to in the Bible. Its little fruits are important to birds as a source of food, and I have seen it attract Purple-rumped Sunbirds which generally feed on nectar and, especially when feeding young, also take insects.

The Lunuwarana (*Crataeva adansonii*) is a tree with a silvery trunk. By the time it has come into bloom it has shed all of its leaves, but it is so densely adorned with flowers that in the distance it could be mistaken for a tree with full foliage. The pale Lunuwarana flowers against a blue sky are richly symbolic of the dry-zone national parks. Another characteristic dry-zone tree is the Divul or Woodapple (*Limonia acidissima*). Its fruit is favoured by humans, with woodapple juice being widely available in supermarkets. Elephants seem partial to it as well, and their consumption of it plays a key role in the dispersal of these trees. The Weera (*Drypetes sepiaria*) is a tree with many branches close to the base like those of a bush; an indecisive tree that has not fully decided what it wants to be. Dictated by soils, there are a few patches in some parks where every tree is a Weera.

The lowland wet zone is, together with the Western Ghats, a global biodiversity hot spot. In Sinharaja about half the trees you see around you are endemic. The tall trees are dominated by dipterocarps (Dipterocarpaceae spp.), whose winged seeds (hence the name dipterocarp, meaning two-winged seed) litter the forest floor when they suddenly bloom. Many of the local guides in Sinharaja know their trees, and a walk with them soon gives you an endemic tree list of 20–30 species within a few hundred metres. Near the entrance gate Purple-faced Leaf Monkeys visit the Jak Trees, with their large, trunk-hugging fruits. The Jak Tree is not found within forests and is believed to be an introduction. Its wild cousin, the Wild Breadfruit (*Artocarpus nobilis*), has deeply lobed leaves and paves the footpath of the Kottawa forest.

Above left: *The flowering of the Lunuwarana is preceded by the tree shedding its leaves.*

Above right: *The Jak Tree is believed to be an introduced species. It has become very important for sustaining populations of the Critically Endangered Western Purple-faced Leaf Monkey in rapidly urbanizing habitats.*

Opposite: *The salt-tolerant Maliththan tree is a characteristic tree in coastal areas of the dry zone. It dominates well-drained, sandy coastal soils in Yala.*

Many of the trees you see in cities are introduced. One of the best examples is the Rain Tree (*Samanea saman*), with its broad, umbrella-shaped canopy. Its name is supposed to come from the noise of caterpillars defecating, which sounds like rain. So far I have not been unfortunate enough to provide first-hand verification. Other common introduced urban trees include the Rusty Shieldbearer (*Peltophorum pterocarpum*) and the Flamboyant (*Delonix regia*). Many of these are in flower in May, and Colombo has earned its tag as a garden city.

The Suriya (*Thespesia populnea*), a small tree with yellow flowers, grows by the roadsides of the dry zone. At river crossings look for the tall and majestic Kumbuk tree, which is adapted to riverine vegetations. Its foliage has a mix of green and red leaves which, together with its pale, flaky bark, make it distinctive.

Flowering plants

Tropical countries have so many plant species that it seems an almost impossible task to provide a brief overview. Sri Lanka is no exception – despite being a small island it has more than 3,500 species of native flowering plant. Therefore this section is written from the perspective of a brief safari guide, starting with Yala National Park as a basis of reference. However, much of what is said about Yala also holds true for most of the parks and reserves in the dry zone.

The casual visitor to the park cannot fail to notice an abundant medium-sized shrub that has yellow flowers in bloom throughout the year. This is the Ranawara (*Cassia auriculata*), whose flowers are dried and drunk as a herbal tea. Dainty, star-shaped white flowers of the Heen-karamba (*Carissa spinarum*) are seen throughout the year lining the roadsides. The Kora Kaha, or Blue Mist (*Memecylon umbellatum*), is a seasonal bloomer. Whorls of blue flowers are tightly clustered along its branches. Horticultural varieties of this plant adorn gardens around the world.

Of the herbaceous plants (those without woody stems), a favourite of mine is the Wara (*Calotropis gigantea*). The milky sap from it is poisonous, but a lot of native insects have co-evolved with it and it is an important plant for insect diversity. The flowers are visited by Carpenter Bees (Xylocopa spp.) and the larvae of some of the tiger butterflies use it as their plant and accumulate toxins from it, making the adults taste bad to predators. The Ath Honda (*Heliotropium indicum*) is a small herb with a flowering peduncle shaped like an elephant's trunk, from which it derives its Sinhala name, meaning elephant's trunk. It is the larval food plant of many species of the tiger butterfly family. Seasonally, there can be clusters of Blues and Dark Blues (*Tirumala limniace leopardus* and *T. septentrionis musikanos*), and Plain and Common Tigers (*Danaus chrysippus* and *D. genutia*) swarming on it. Here again, the caterpillars ingest alkaloids that make the adults taste bad to predators.

Horton Plains National Park is a good place to see highland plants. The first thing to note is that the most obvious flowering plants are invasive species. The

Left: *The Ranawara is found in bloom year-round in the dry lowlands. Its flowers are dried and made into a herbal drink.*

Opposite top: *The two Rain Trees (*Samanea saman*) and the Water Hyacinth (*Eichhornia crassipes*) are examples of how introduced plants dominate some of the cultivated landscapes.*

Opposite below: *The Kumbuk is a water-loving tree, common beside rivers. Old trees can grow to an enormous girth.*

Above: The Kora Kaha has synchronized flowering in the dry zone, forming avenues lined with blue.

Right: Caterpillars of tiger butterflies feed on the Wara and ingest poisonous alkaloids which make them taste bad. The flowers are also popular with other insects.

Below right: Wild Ginger is a common rainforest plant. Its flowers may be an important source of nectar.

Opposite: Pitcher plants attract insects inside to a sugary fluid at the bottom of the pitcher. The insects cannot climb back up the slippery walls so they drown; nitrates from their bodies are then absorbed by the plants.

Gorse (*Ulex europeaus*) was deliberately introduced by European planters and is now the target of removal programmes. The white-flowered Common Floss Flower (*Eupatorum odoratum*) is yet another invasive plant, which lines the roadsides in the hills. One of the specialities of the plains is the Dwarf Bamboo (*Arundinaria densifolia*). The plains also have many species of Strobilanthes that are famous for their synchronized mass flowering. *Lobelia nicotianifolia*, with its long flowering spikes, is a distinctive plant in the highlands. Swampy areas of Horton Plains National Park are dominated by the Dwarf Bamboo, with the drier areas having tussock grasses of species of *Chrysopogon* and *Garnotia*.

Many of the paths in the wet zone are lined with plants of an invasive bowitiya (*Melastoma malabathricum*). The deeply corrugated leaves maximize the surface area to capture sunlight in the same way as our wrinkled brain cortex maximizes its surface area. The enhanced light capture makes the plant an aggressive competitor, but it is nevertheless confined to open areas. There are several other species of bowitiya (*Osbeckia* spp.), with pink flowers. The plants grow on roadsides from the Kotte Marshes to Sinharaja and Horton Plains. The *Osbeckia* and *Melastoma* genera both belong to the same plant family (Melastomataceae).

Road journeys provide ample plant-spotting opportunities. In the wet zone the roads are lined with the dainty blue-flowering spikes of Balu Nakuta (*Stachytarpheta jamaicensis*). There are several similar-looking species, some of which are native. The one commonly seen is an introduced species, but the native fauna have taken to it. A common invasive plant is the Gandapana (*Lantana camara*), originally from Central America. In some national parks, like Uda Walawe, expensive eradication programmes have been carried out to prevent it from taking over swathes of ground by stifling the local flora. One thing in its favour is that the local butterflies nectar extensively on it. A common local plant also favoured by butterflies is the Pagoda-flower (*Clerodendrum paniculatum*). Its flowers have deep funnels and butterflies that drink from them have long probosces.

The most famous species in Sinharaja are the insectivorous pitcher plants called Bandura (*Nepenthes distillatoria*), which are found in disturbed soils where the nutrients have been leached away by water. Anywhere built or cleared, like the old logging roadsides, is a good place to see them. The plants use insects to obtain the nitrates that are absent in the soil, and are able to colonize areas in which other plants cannot gain a tendril hold. The Spiral Ginger (*Costus speciosus*) is a common herbaceous plant in the rainforest ground storey. *Freycenetia walkeri*, an endemic with prominent red fruit, is a climber on large tree trunks. Sinharaja also has a few species of endemic rattan (*Calamus* spp.), conspicuous plants for their height and palm-like leaves.

Night Safaris

Night safaris taken to look for nocturnal animals can be rewarding experiences, but should always be done with your personal safety and the welfare of the animals in mind. It is also necessary to take into account the concerns of the state conservation agencies. If you are using a spotlight or powerful torch, remember never to shine it directly into the eyes of nocturnal animals. Always have the animals off-centre in the beam so that they are not dazzled by it. Shining a torch directly at an animal can cause eye damage if the light is powerful. Avoid using a white light, which animals are sensitive to. Always use a red light, which does not bother animals. Even a weak light covered with a red filter will throw back enough 'eye-shine' for nocturnal animals to be seen. The soft red light will not result in animals being disturbed or harmed by the light, and it is much better than a powerful white light for obtaining views of nocturnal animals.

The Fauna and Flora Protection Ordinance was originally drafted with several anti-hunting clauses in it. These have been retained in subsequent revisions. One of these relates to prohibitions on spotlighting animals. The original concern would have been that if someone was spotlighting an animal, the intention would have been to shoot it. This piece of legislation has been used by game rangers to stop people from looking at animals (including birds such as nightjars) using torches and spotlights. On one occasion a group of visitors was travelling on a major 'A road' and shining torches into a protected area that the road ran through. The group was stopped and the vehicle was impounded. However, incidents such as this are rare. The majority of field staff of the two main conservation agencies are doing their best to do a good job under difficult circumstances. Most will go out of their way to help.

If you intend to look for nocturnal animals even on a public road near or passing through a protected area,

speak to the officials of the nearest office of the Forest Department or Department of Wildlife Conservation and explain your intentions. They may even send someone along to assist you. If you are at a forest, village or cultural site, even if there is public access in the night for the forested trail you will be on, avoid suspicion by explaining to the locals what you are going to be doing. At a few sites people have become accustomed to birders coming in search of animals such as nightjars and owls.

In the thorn-scrub forests of the dry zone, night-walkers are potentially at risk from elephants. An injured crop-raiding elephant is an irascible animal that can kill. Sudden encounters with Sloth Bears and Water Buffalos could also be dangerous. Kraits (*Bungarus* spp.), cobras and vipers are active at night. Stout shoes and long trousers minimize the risk of a fatally venomous snakebite. Forest trails can also have 'trap guns' set on them. Unless a forest trail is regularly used as a public footpath, it is best not to use it without enlisting the help of a local who is familiar with the area.

There is good-quality forest near the entrance gates of some of the cultural sites. After having a friendly chat with the security staff, I have often been allowed to walk outside the perimeter with a soft red light, with the comfort of being able to leave my vehicle under the care of the staff.

Top: The Common Palm Civet has badger-like black and pale markings on its face, found in many nocturnal hunters, to help break up its outline.

*Centre: Giant Flying Squirrels (*Petaurista philippensis*) become tame and elicit wonder as they glide across surprising distances.*

Right: The Serendib Scops-owl has an anatomical adaptation on its legs which makes it easy for it to perch on thin vertical stems.

Opposite: Ring-tailed Civets are common nocturnal hunters found from urban habitats in the lowlands to the cloud forests.

Underwater Life

Sri Lanka has 1,700 km (1,055 miles) of coastline. A huge number of marine wildlife species is present here, including invertebrates and vertebrates. This section focuses on the larger, relatively easily seen animals, especially the fish that one may see in both the sea and fresh water. Note that it does not cover whales, dolphins and other marine mammals, which are described in their own section (see page 104).

Marine Species

There are many opportunities for rock pooling, and guided rock-pooling excursions are available. Sri Lanka still lacks a comprehensive marine-wildlife guide, partly because there are so many species. However, regional guides to fish, seashells, and so on can be used by visitors to identify many of the commonly seen species if they choose to rock pool or snorkel. Rock pools are good places to see mudskippers (subfamily Oxudercinae), which are found in both coastal and marine environments. They can breathe air directly, enabling them to survive above the water. Various species of crab can be seen on the shoreline, including hermit crabs (*Paguroidea* spp.), which shelter inside abandoned seashells.

According to the data on www.fishbase.org, at the time of writing 954 species of marine fish had been recorded in Sri Lanka, with 570 species associated with reefs. There are probably many more species to be recorded, and some may even be new to science.

Divers are spoiled for choice in Sri Lanka's coastal waters. However, these waters do not enjoy the strong reputation for diving as do some other tropical diving destinations such as the Maldives. One reason for this may be that the monsoons and 105 river systems contribute to a lot of sediment and nutrient run-off, so that clear water is only available for limited periods and at times a fair distance away from shore. However, the island has extensive fringing coral reefs, and its marine life has not received the coverage it deserves.

The nutrient run-off contributes to the presence of a rich food chain in coastal waters, which sustains a population of whales throughout the year. Other large plankton feeders such as the Whale Shark (*Rhincodon typus*) are present here – I have seen this species on whale-watching trips from both Mirissa and Trincomalee. Sometime rays (Batoidea spp.) are also seen close to shore and may be observed from whale-watching boats. Rex de Silva, a diver and naturalist, has prepared a checklist of sharks and rays recorded off Sri Lanka that includes 61 species of shark and 31 species of ray. No sharks are known to have attacked humans off Sri Lanka.

The bottom half of the west coast is highly developed for tourism and many of the resort areas have dive operators. Some of the better established areas for diving are Beruwela, Bentota, Hikkaduwa and Unawatuna. The last is also very good for snorkelling. A number of glass-bottomed boat operators offer excursions to the Hikkaduwa Marine National Park. They provide good opportunities for general visitors to see some of the reef life without getting their feet wet.

***Above:** Many species of stone coral can be seen in the Barr Reef Sanctuary off the Kalpitiya Peninsula.*

***Opposite:** Oval Butterflyfish* (Chaetodon trifasciatus) *travel in shoals in search of live coral to feed on.*

In the northern half of the island Negombo has a strip of hotels, with several having dive operators. Further north in the Kalpitiya Peninsula is the Sperm Whale line. At the northern end is the famous Barr Reef. Many people go snorkelling here – unfortunately the reef is badly damaged due to careless visitation in the shallower sections.

The east coast is opening up for divers. Its dive sites include the wreck of the aircraft carrier *Hermes*, involving technical dives to be attempted only by the very experienced. Viewing marine life can be done easily from China Bay, or by taking a boat ride to Pigeon Island. The coral around Pigeon Island has been damaged by visitors, but it is still possible to see many species of fish. A famous dive site on the south-east is the Great Basses, with a short dive window in April, although conditions are sometimes only good for diving here for 2–4 weeks. The continental shelf extends far out from the shore to the dive site near the Great Basses Lighthouse. Because of the extent of the shelf, the water here is too shallow to offer good chances for seeing whales. However, dolphins may be spotted around boats.

Top: *A close look is needed to see the scalpel-like spine on this Palette Surgeonfish (*Paracanthurus hepatus*). It is a herbivore with specialized gut bacteria.*

Centre: *Schooling Bannerfinfish (*Heniochus diphreutes*) are butterflyfish with elongated dorsal fins.*

Right: *Anthias are related to groupers. The females do not have the long thread-like extension at the front of the dorsal fin and can change sex to become males.*

Freshwater Fish

At the present time, Sri Lanka is known to have 72 species of native fish whose adult lives are confined to fresh water. Of these species, 38 are endemic. About half the endemic fish have been described by Rohan Pethiyagoda and his team at the Wildlife Heritage Trust in the last few decades. According to records in www.fishbase.org, a further 21 introduced freshwater species are present. Some of the endemic species can be seen easily from stream-sides in Sinharaja and Morapitiya. Just before the turn-off to the Morapitiya forest reserve at Athwelthota there is a bathing spot on the river that runs parallel to the road. This is also a good place to see some of the endemic species. The streams that cross the main road in Kottawa Rainforest and Arboretum in the Galle District are also good places in which to see stream fish.

Typical stream fish include Cherry Barbs (*Puntius titteya*) and Striped Rasbora (*Rasbora daniconius*). In Sinharaja the stream near the research station is a good place in which to see the Paradise Combtail (*Belontia signata*), with its beautiful red tail. Looking nondescript are the Stone Suckers (*Garra phillipsi*), which use suckers to attach themselves to the surfaces of rocks. The enigmatic Dwarf Killifish (*Aplocheilus parvus*) are widespread in streams and ditches. The adults can lay their eggs in ephemeral pools and may die. The eggs survive the seasonal drying and hatch when the next rains arrive. Seemingly miraculously, pools that were once dry are now filled with fish sporting a moon crescent on the forehead, giving rise to a local name, '*handaya*', meaning moon. Killifish can also leap out of a pool when threatened, and wriggle over land to other pools.

Top: *Males of the endemic Paradise Combtail species have rays trailing from the tail fin. Its numbers have reduced due to its being captured for export to collectors.*

Right: *The Dwarf Killifish is one of three killifish found in Sri Lanka. The other two are endemic.*

Hiyare Rainforest for Endemic Fish

22 November

We inspected two streams just before Hiyare. The first contained mainly Kelum's Barb (*Puntius kelumi*), easily distinguished from the Striped Rasbora because it lacks a side stripe. The Kelum's Barb in the stream showed a red caudal fin with a black spot at the base. This species has been split from the Long-snouted Barb (*Puntius dorsalis*), which has also been recorded in the wet zone but is not as brightly coloured. Striped Rasbora and a few endemic Sinhala Barb (*Puntius sinhala*) were also present.

The next stream is the one that runs under the bridge just before the turn-off to the Hiyare Centre. It was in full flow. In the shallow, near-stagnant pool connected to it were juveniles of the endemic Cherry Barb. I was told that this was a typical breeding pool for the species. The Hiyare Reservoir had the usual large shoal of Sinhala Barb. A few adult males had the filamented dorsal fin that gave rise to the species' earlier name of Filamented Barb.

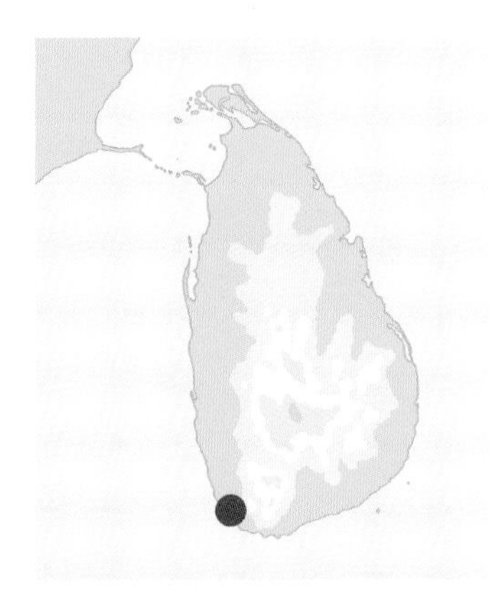

Opposite: *The Hiyare Rainforest managed by the Galle Municipality is a good example of local authorities encouraging education about and access to rainforests.*

Below left: *The common Striped Rasbora is easily identified by its black lateral band.*

Below: *The female Cherry Barb is less brightly coloured than the male. This endemic fish has been depleted by collection for the aquarium trade.*

4
Whales, Dolphins and Seabirds

The charismatic Blue Whale and Sperm Whale, as well as dolphins, porpoises and the Dugong – 27 marine mammal species in total – inhabit Sri Lankan waters. A large variety of seabirds and fish, including the largest fish in the world, the Whale Shark, can also be seen around the coast.

Left: *Spinner Dolphins in Kalpitiya porpoise as they travel at high speed. Note the young one keeping close to its mother.*

Whale-watching Locations

There are three key locations for whale watching, all characterized by the presence of deep water close to shore. They are Mirissa, Trincomalee and Kalpitiya, and are described below.

Trincomalee has been mooted as a whale-watching location since the 1980s, but it was not until April 2010, following the end of the separatist war, that commercial whale watching began here. Kalpitiya's development for whale watching began in February 2010, although it had become known for its Spinner Dolphins by 2009. Its claim as a whale-watching site was corroborated by seismic exploration data that became available in January 2010. This showed that the continental shelf was closer than had been depicted in the admiralty charts.

Twenty-six species of cetacean (whales and dolphins) and the Dugong (*Dugong dugon*) have been recorded in Sri Lankan waters, giving a total of 27 marine mammal species. On a dedicated whale-watching tour, which includes five to seven sailings, it is possible to see five or six species.

Mirissa

Fully fledged commercial whale watching was first developed in Mirissa, in southern Sri Lanka. It followed on from a massive publicity campaign (backed by field data) in May 2008, drawing on a hypothesis by British marine biologist Dr Charles Anderson. The Anderson hypothesis is that Blue Whales seen off Sri Lanka's east coast are migrating between the Arabian Sea (off the Horn of Africa) and the Bay of Bengal. This would see them passing close to Dondra, the southernmost point in Sri Lanka, travelling east in around November–December and west (on the return journey) in late March and April. Dr Anderson set out on his first trip in April 2007, and saw Blue Whales from the Dondra Lighthouse as well as out at sea. Since then, on some sailings as many as 17 individual Blue Whales have been recorded. On one exceptional occasion in November 2010, more than 25 Blue Whales were seen as they migrated into Sri Lankan waters. However, it should be noted that many counts by inexperienced observers exaggerate numbers by miscounting repeat sightings as distinct individuals. On several occasions at least five Blue Whales have been in my field of view simultaneously, and on a handful of occasions I saw four Blue Whales within a 300 m (984 ft) radius of the boat.

The continental shelf pinches in close (5.5 km/ 3 miles) to shore at Dondra, which is near to the fishery harbour at Mirissa. The proximity of deep water and the nutrient flow at the edge of the continental shelf is a key factor for whales and oceanic dolphins being seen close to shore. Blue Whales are often seen within an hour of sailing.

Timing Whale watching starts in late October or early November, once the seas have calmed after the south-west monsoon. The best viewing period is from December to mid-April.

Whales and dolphins On a single sailing between December and mid-April, there is a 90 per cent chance of seeing a Blue Whale – a higher encounter rate than that for the next most likely species to be seen, the Spinner Dolphin. Sperm Whales are the next most frequently recorded species. It is possible that Common Bottlenose Dolphins (*Tursiops truncatus*) are encountered more regularly, but are overlooked. They are often seen close to the harbour and sometimes further out to sea. At times they bow ride. Other dolphins that are seen here include Pantropical Spotted Dolphins (*Stenella attenuata*), which sometimes bow ride boats in the same way that Spinner Dolphins do, and Striped Dolphins (*Stenella coeruleoalba*).

Opposite: The blow or spout of the Blue Whale can be as much as three storeys high.

Below: The fishery harbour of Mirissa with its collection of colourful boats witnessed the launch of a commercial whale-watching industry in May 2008.

In May 2008, I photographed what was then believed to be a pair of Humpback Whales (*Megaptera novaeangliae*) in the distance but I now believe they were probably Blue Whales, perhaps engaged in a courtship chase. Therefore there is as yet no reliable recent record of Humpback Whales. In January 2013, there was an observation of a suspected Sei Whale (*Balenoptera borealis*) followed by another off Kalpitiya in February 2013. Orcas (*Orcinus orca*) are very rare, but now that every day in the season is being sailed, records of Orcas have increased from one encounter every two years to up to four a year. Pods of Short-finned Pilot Whales (*Globicephala macrorhynchus*) appear occasionally. On one occasion I saw Bryde's, Blue and Sperm Whales in the space of half an hour, but this is unusual. On two successive sailings with Dr Anderson, I saw seven species of cetacean. Again, this is unusual, and the chances of seeing more species

are improved when you are with an expert. However, cetaceans can be seen on almost every sailing.

The 14 species of cetacean recorded from Mirissa are as follows: Blue Whale, Bryde's Whale, Sperm Whale, Orca (Killer Whale), False Killer Whale (*Pseudorca crassidens*), Melon-headed Whale (*Peponocephala electra*), Short-finned Pilot Whale, Risso's Dolphin (*Grampus griseus*), Rough-toothed Dolphin (*Steno bredanensis*), Common Bottlenose Dolphin, Fraser's Dolphin (*Lagenodelphis hosei*), Spinner Dolphin, Pantropical Spotted Dolphin and Striped Dolphin.

Other sea animals The Whale Shark and Manta Ray (*Manta birostris*) are occasionally encountered near the mouth of Weligama Bay. Sun Fish (*Mola mola*) have also been seen, and there have been regular sightings of flying fish (Exocoetidae spp.). Green, Olive Ridley and Loggerhead Turtles are occasionally encountered.

Seabirds The most exciting time for seabirds is around late March to mid-April, just before the onset of the south-west monsoon. Unfortunately this is also the time when the sea becomes progressively rougher.

Pomarine and Parasitic (Arctic) Skuas (*Stercorarius pomarinus* and *S. parasiticus*) appear at this time. Usually you need to be about 18–30 km (10–15 miles) out to sea to view these birds. On one sailing with Dr Anderson we saw a flock of 17 Pomarine Skuas, which brought our total tally for the day to 42. Flesh-footed and Wedge-tailed Shearwaters (*Puffinus carneipes* and *P. pacificus*) also arrive at this time, and on a single sailing over a dozen sightings may be had. Noddies – possibly both Lesser and Brown Noddies (*Anous tenuirostris tenuirostris* and *A. stolidus pileatus*) – are occasionally seen with flocks of other terns.

Other rarities that have been recorded here include Red-billed and White-tailed Tropicbirds (*Phaethon aethereus indicus* and *P. lepturus lepturus*), and the Sooty Shearwater (*Puffinus griseus*). The Brown-winged or Bridled Tern (*Onychoprion anaethetus*) is a pelagic seabird rarely seen by shore-based birdwatchers, but is easy to view throughout the season from the whale-watching boats. Other seabirds seen here regularly include Little Terns, and Great Crested and Lesser Crested Terns (*Sterna bergii* and *S. bengalensis bengalensis*). White-winged Black Terns and Whiskered Terns (*Chlidonias hybridus hybridus*) are birds that winter inland, but as they prepare for the return migration flocks gather by the shoreline. White-winged Black Terns form flocks that hunt over the sea. The migration patterns of the seabirds differ during the March–April period: the 'marsh terns' will be moving north; the Brown-winged Tern may be on a return migration to south-west Australia; the shearwaters are flying west to the Arabian Sea, and the Pomarine Skuas appear to be flying east to the Bay of Bengal.

Left: *A Wedge-tailed Shearwater skims the ocean's surface off Kalpitiya. In rough seas, they glide effortlessly, shearing the waves'*

Opposite top: *Microfolds on a dolphin's skin help reduce friction, allowing it to travel at speed through water.*

Opposite below: *Striped Dolphins occasionally play with boats and will breach.*

Opposite: A Blue Whale off Trincomalee shows the broad tail flukes that can span 4.5 m (15 ft).

Below: Swami Rock in Trincomalee is the best shore-based lookout point for seeing Blue Whales.

Trincomalee

Swami Rock, which has the Koneswaram Temple atop it, is the best shore-based location in the world for seeing Blue Whales. Sperm Whales are also at times seen from Swami Rock. Trincomalee has a submarine canyon that comes into the land, creating a deep natural harbour. This also provides the conditions for the occurrence of whales close to shore. Boats from the resorts to the north of the harbour reach Blue Whale feeding locations within half an hour.

Trincomalee had been held out as a location for whale watching since the 1980s. However, a proper assessment of its commercial feasibility for whale watching, led by the Nature Trails team of John Keells from Chaaya Blu, did not begin until April 2010. Initially the view was that after April almost all of the Blue Whales would have migrated back to the Arabian Sea. Therefore the resorts did not offer whale watching between late April and September. However, it has recently been established that there are sufficient numbers of Blue and Sperm Whales still present to make commercial whale watching feasible from May to September. Sri Lanka therefore now has a commercial whale-watching season of 9–10 months.

Timing The north-east monsoon occurs from October to February. The whale-watching season begins in March as the seas become calmer. Between March and the first week of April, Trincomalee has the added benefit of migratory Blue Whales that are still present. In one year the encounter rate was more than 95 per cent, but in the following year it dropped dramatically. After mid-April the combined encounter rate for Blue and Sperm Whales is about 80 per cent to August. The encounter rates are volatile and more data is required.

Whales and dolphins The species to be seen off Trincomalee are similar to those seen off Mirissa. During March 2012, naturalists Nilantha Kodithuwakku and B. Dayarathne from Chaaya Blu observed a large pod of Sperm Whales estimated at 60 to 200 individuals. Kodituwakku counted 40

full-body breaches in one morning. I saw a wide repertoire of Sperm Whale social behaviour off Trincomalee in April 2012. The large concentrations of Sperm Whales in Sri Lankan waters have been commented on as being special by many foreign researchers who have engaged in cetacean research elsewhere in the world. At the present time, the number of species recorded is less than what it could be because commercial whale watching, which began here in April 2012, is relatively new, and to date there have been very few specialist naturalists going out to sea. For example, the first confirmed sighting of an Orca occurred as recently as September 2012.

The following 13 species of cetacean have been recorded off Trincomalee since April 2010: Sperm Whale, Dwarf Sperm Whale, Longman's Beaked Whale (*Indopacetus pacificus*), Orca (Killer Whale), False Killer Whale, Risso's Dolphin, Common Bottlenose Dolphin, Common Dolphin (*Delphinus delphis*), Spinner Dolphin, Pantropical Spotted Dolphin, Striped Dolphin, Blue Whale and Bryde's Whale.

Other sea animals I encountered a Whale Shark on one trip. It seemed very comfortable with boats and swam up to and spent time with the boat.

Seabirds The seabirds in this location are similar to those at Mirissa and Kalpitiya. To date, very few birders have been at sea here, so the species list is relatively thin. Brown-winged Terns are at times seen relatively close to shore. In April 2012 I found that shearwaters and skuas were absent from Trincomalee, when only a few days earlier they had been seen in Kalpitiya. This could be due to the nutrient-rich upwellings that occur at this time of the year on the west coast, where Kalpitiya is situated.

Kalpitiya

Although Blue Whales are largely absent from Kalpitya, it is a reliable location for Sperm Whales, especially between March and April. Kalpitiya first came into the spotlight in 2008 and 2009, when resort operators reported large schools of Spinner Dolphins. These were daytime sightings of dolphins resting or sleeping inshore off a nearby reef. Kalpitya's potential for commercial whale watching was not explored until February 2011, when I set out to specifically look for whales. The admiralty charts available at that time suggested that the continental shelf was far away. However, I was given access to new sea-floor data that had been mapped in October 2009 and published in January 2010. It showed that the shelf ran parallel and close to shore. This explained why oceanic species like Spinner Dolphins and Sperm Whales were being seen as close as 15 minutes away by speedboat.

Timing As in the case of Mirissa, the boats start whale watching once the seas calm after the south-west monsoon. The period between December and mid-April is good for going out to sea. Data remains sparse on whales, although Sperm Whales have been recorded in February, and fairly regularly in March and April. Rare pelagic seabirds are seen in April, when the seas start to turn rough with the onset of the south-west monsoon.

Opposite: *A Sperm Whale off Kalpitiya swam up to our boat, went alongside it, then began a feeding dive from just a few metres away. The smooth flukes suggest the accident-free history of a young whale.*

Below: *A Sperm Whale commences a feeding dive off Kalpitiya.*

Whales and dolphins Kalpitiya has an advantage in that pelagic seabirds and Sperm Whales are both seen in the same location, in a band that is approximately between E 79 35 and E 79 38. In sites such as Kaikoura off New Zealand, birdwatchers often do not see Sperm Whales because the whale watching is carried out further offshore in deeper water. In Kalpitiya, the birds and whales are both seen roughly following a north–south axis along the 400 m (1,300 ft) depth isobath, which is rich in food. Moreover, in Kalpitiya as in Mirissa, Sperm Whales are seen in pods that can number up to 50 or more. Most typically, one encounters a pod where up to about seven whales may be seen simultaneously on the surface.

Spinner Dolphins are the most common cetacean seen off the peninsula. They are usually encountered inshore of the reef on the Dolphin line (closer to shore than the Sperm Whale line), where they rest during the day. There are regular claims of sightings of super-pods numbering more than 2,000 Spinner Dolphins; such large pods are not seen anywhere else in Sri Lanka. A pod I once encountered stretched over 2 km (1¼ miles).

At present it is not clear why Blue Whales are rarely seen off Kalpitiya. It may be that the Blue Whales that are resident in Sri Lankan waters move from the east coast to locations such as Kalpitiya to benefit from the upwelling created by the south-west monsoon. This would coincide with the close of the whale-watching season. Sightings of Blue Whales in April give credence to this theory.

In the early days the few scattered observations of whales came from dolphin watchers who had unwittingly crossed over the reef to the Sperm Whale line. Cetaceans recorded off the Kalpitiya Peninsula include the Blue Whale, Bryde's Whale, Minke Whale

(*Balaenoptera bonaerensis*), Dwarf Sperm Whale (*Kogia simia*), Cuvier's Beaked Whale (*Ziphius cavirostris*), Melon-headed Whale, Killer Whale (Orca), False Killer Whale, Short-finned Pilot Whale, Risso's Dolphin, Rough-toothed Dolphin, Indo-Pacific Humpback Dolphin (*Sousa chinensis*), Common Bottlenose Dolphin, Fraser's Dolphin, Pantropical Spotted Dolphin and Striped Dolphin. I suspect that Kalpitiya may be the best location for Bryde's Whale in Sri Lanka. More species will be recorded as more skilled observers start watching cetaceans off Kalpitiya. This area also seems to be the best site in Sri Lanka for the Orca, with at least one or two records each year. To see the Indo-Pacific Humpback Dolphin, a special trip has to be arranged to the mouth of the Puttalam Lagoon.

Other sea animals There is an abundance of flying fish, which must be a further clue to the rich food chain here around the 400 m (1,300 ft) depth isobath. The fishing boats also haul in large specimens of Yellow-fin Tuna (*Thunnus albacares*). Green and Olive Ridley Turtles have been seen at sea as well as in the extensive Puttalam Lagoon. The Whale Shark is also occasionally encountered. The nearby Barr Reef is one of the richest coral reefs in Asia.

Left and below: *Spinner Dolphins travelling at speed using a technique called porpoising. Observed from a boat, it was difficult to understand the dynamics and know why extra speed was needed.*

Opposite: *Spinner Dolphins engage in short bursts of speed chases. These could be displays of fitness or could just be engaged in for fun.*

Above: *An exhausted juvenile Sooty Tern rests after a heavy storm the day before.*

Top: *A Common Tern uses floating debris to rest on.*

Seabirds Many seabirds can be seen off the Kalpitiya Peninsula. Hunting along the coastlines are Gull-billed Terns. Lesser Crested and Large Crested Terns are often seen in mixed tern flocks that include Gull-billed as well as Little Terns and, less frequently, Common Terns. I have often seen flocks of Little Terns in the food-rich areas between E 79 35 and E 79 38. On the beach you may see Whiskered and White-winged Black Terns. Both species are migrant marsh terns and are rarely seen over the sea. However, flocks of White-winged Black Terns gather to feed at sea off Mirissa at the tail end of the migration. There are a few records of exhausted Sooty Terns (*Sterna fuscata nubilosa*) landing on the beach. Bridled Terns (*Onychoprion anaethetus*) are pelagic birds seasonally seen in good numbers. Unless there is bad weather, they rarely venture close to shore.

The area between E 79 35 and E 79 38 seems to be one of the best places for seeing Lesser and Brown Noddies. Most observers in Sri Lanka have found them hard to find, but once when I was on a trip in Kalpitiya with Riaz Cader, a Lesser Noddy even attempted to land on our boat. We also photographed a Long-tailed Skua (*Stercorarius longicaudus*) – this may be confirmed as the second record of this species in Sri Lanka and one of the first few for the Indian subcontinent. Although I have photographed the Pomarine Skua here, I have not seen it in the numbers in which it is seen off Mirissa. In April 2010 I saw a flock of more than 35 Persian Shearwaters (*Puffinus persicus*) – perhaps the third record of this species from Sri Lanka, although this is yet to be confirmed. Persian Shearwaters were also photographed in April 2011 and April 2012, and it seems April is the time to see them off Kalpitiya.

Flesh-footed and Wedge-tailed Shearwaters also join some of the mixed-species seabird feeding flocks. I have glimpsed petrels but have not been able to identify them. On 15 January 2012, Riaz Cader went out to sea and photographed a rarely recorded Brown Booby (*Sula leucogaster*). The Brown-headed Gull (*Larus brunnicephalus*), a winter visitor that is variable in numbers, has also been recorded here. The nearby salt pans at Puttalam usually contain a few Caspian Terns, which make an occasional appearance in Kalpitiya. The area over the 400 m (1,300 ft) isobath offshore from Kandakuliya seems to be a pelagic-bird 'sweet spot' – perhaps due to a confluence of nutrients from different sources, which create a rich zone of marine life. The 400 m (1,300 ft) isobath also comes closer to shore as you move north along the peninsula. This explains why whales and pelagic seabirds are seen close to Kandakuliya and the Barr Reef.

Below left: *A Lesser Noddy; a scarce pelagic bird.*

Below right: *Bridled or Brown-winged Terns in breeding plumage show tail streamers.*

Bottom: *A Brown Noddy on the water shows its heavy, dagger-like bill.*

Above: A Long-tailed Skua resting on the water off Kalpitiya was the second record for Sri Lanka.

Right: I have seen scores of Persian Shearwaters off Kalpitiya; this is a species that hitherto had been recorded just once.

Above: A juvenile Pomarine Skua uses rigifoam debris for resting.

Top: Wedge-tailed Shearwaters arrive at the onset of the south-west monsoon. They rest on the water.

Some Whale Facts

Origins of Blue Whales

The Blue Whales seen off Sri Lanka adopt two feeding strategies. Some undertake an east–west migration between the Arabian Sea off the Horn of Africa and the Bay of Bengal. They are seen travelling east off Mirissa in around November to December, and travelling west on the return migration in around March to April. Until September 2011 it was believed that the majority of Blue Whales seen off Trincomalee were migrants, and that the number of resident Blue Whales was not sufficient to support a viable whale-watching industry. As already mentioned, we now know that there are enough resident Blue Whales off Trincomalee to make whale watching feasible all the way through from December to August before the arrival of the north-east monsoon. However, from April, there is a reduction in numbers as the migrants that arrived in November and December from the Arabian Sea have left. At this stage there is insufficient data to assess the numbers of Blue Whales and whether individuals alternate between migratory and resident feeding strategies. Photographic identification of individual whales will allow the population dynamics to be better understood. When it comes to Sperm Whales, their pattern is more complex and it is too early to speculate on their movements.

Watching Cetaceans

The same rules of common sense apply to almost all animals if you wish to enjoy an extended and possibly close sighting.

- Never bear down rapidly on any animal at any angle. Even an animal used to people and vehicles will take fright. Do not approach marine mammals head on or from behind.

- Do not chase whales and dolphins from behind to try and get a rear-view 'tail shot'. Approach them in parallel and keep at a distance comfortable to them (at least 100 m/300 ft away). If you cut off the engine they may sometimes swim up to the boat for a closer look out of curiosity. They may then dive away from you, providing the popular tail shot.

- Whales and dolphins in Sri Lanka's three key whale-watching sites are very used to fishing boats and ships, and may surface only a few metres away from boats. However, the decision to get close to a boat has to be theirs. Do not follow them for an extended period as they are not used to being pursued. Furthermore, boat noise will stress the animals as they rely on sensitive hearing for communication and – in the case of some species – for hunting. Dolphins may choose to bow ride, but they are unlikely to do so if you chase them.

Whale Sightings

Cetaceans are mammals and need to surface to breathe air. A feeding Blue Whale engaged in shallow dives may surface every 10 to 12 minutes. Similarly, Sperm Whales on shallow dives may surface every 15 to 20 minutes, but can stay underwater for an hour. People often count the same whale multiple times, so a report of 20 Blue Whales may actually refer to five individuals, each of which was seen surfacing an average of four times. Most people lack the experience to make a reasonably accurate estimate of the total number of individuals encountered on a trip, because both the whales and the boat are in motion, creating confusion in assessing the number of animals. The number of whale spouts (or blows) that can be seen simultaneously is often the best indication of how many whales are present. However, not all reports of multiple Blue Whales are the results of confusion between sightings versus individuals. On one occasion, on 5 November 2010, naturalist Anoma Alagiyawadu was on a sailing boat that observed a group of more than 25 Blue Whales travelling together. On some days an experienced observer such as Dr Anderson has seen an estimated 17 unique individuals within a 5 km (3 mile) quadrat off Mirissa. For comparison, on the same day from another boat, I could see a maximum of five Blue Whales spouting simultaneously.

Whale Identification

To study the behaviour of any animal, it is useful to identify individuals uniquely. In the case of whales, a combination of characteristics is used – mainly patterns on the tail flukes, with dorsal fins as a secondary characteristic. Some Sperm Whales show distinctive calluses on their dorsal fins. These are believed to occur on older females. The best way to track whales is by using radio tags. If a comprehensive photo catalogue of Blue and Sperm Whales seen off Sri Lanka could be built, it would shed much light on their behaviour. For example, do some Blue Whales remain in Sri Lankan waters in some years and migrate in others, or do the whales that stay and those that migrate remain either residents or migrants?

Above: *Calluses develop on adult female Sperm Whales and are a secondary sexual characteristic.*

LOCATION DETAILS SUMMARY		
Time and Encounter Rate	Blues Whales–Resident vs. Migrant*	Rough Seas
MIRISSA		
Blue Whales November–mid-April. December–January, Blue Whales migrating east to Bay of Bengal and return migration to Arabian Sea (Horn of Africa) in April–March. 90 per cent encounter rate in season. **Sperm Whales** Ad hoc throughout season. Super-pods are not common.	Outside the migratory period, the seas are too rough to look for resident Blue Whales.	South-west monsoon: May–September. Inter-monsoonal October. Calming from November. Turns rough in mid-April.
TRINCOMALEE		
Blue Whales March–April, maximum numbers of Blue Whales because of migrants. Variable, some years as high as 90 per cent encounter rate. May–September, resident Blue Whales. **Sperm Whales** March–April, super-pods have been recorded. Data still thin. May–August, Trincomalee has a combined encounter rate which has been as high as 80% for Blue and Sperm Whales.	Migrant and resident Blue Whales. May–September, resident Blue Whales.	North-east monsoon: October–February. Seas calm from March to late September.
KALPITIYA		
Blue Whales Rarely seen. **Sperm Whales** Most reliable site in Sri Lanka for Sperm Whales. December–mid-April. Encounter rate from 1 in 3 to 1 in 5, but data is still thin. March–April, super-pods have been recorded. **Bryde's Whale** May be the most reliable site. Encounter rate of 1 in 5. **Orca** Seems to be recorded every year. Best site in Sri Lanka, but too infrequent for searches to be carried out. **Dugong** Whale watchers have encountered it, but too infrequent for searches to be carried out.	Resident Blue Whales may be present during south-west monsoon, but seas are too rough to look for them.	South-west monsoon: May–September. Inter-monsoonal October. Calming from November. Turns rough in mid-April.

*Migrant vs. resident Blue Whales: Blue Whales that choose to feed in Sri Lankan waters are referred to as residents as opposed to the migrants that travel to the Arabian Sea during the south-west monsoon (May–September).

Surface Behaviour of Cetaceans

This section describes more than 30 elements of the behavioural repertoire of cetaceans, and other facts relevant to behaviour. Knowing the vocabulary for the animals' surface behaviour and understanding what is observed can enrich a whale-watching trip. All of the behaviour below has been observed in Sri Lankan waters, but bear in mind that some of it is rarely seen.

There are other behaviours, such as bubble-netting and skim feeding, which are not described here because they are not likely to be seen in Sri Lankan waters.

Belly-up Cetaceans occasionally lie on their backs. This is rarely seen behaviour, although whales are known to perform belly-ups during bouts of social behaviour. It is believed that females may also do this to avoid the unwanted attentions of males. Both males and females do belly-ups for different reasons.

Blow (spout) Whales, being mammals, need to come up to air to breathe. The blow is their exhalation on the surface. Some species can be identified by their characteristic blows. Blue Whale blows are tall and columnar. Sperm Whale blows are low and bushy, and are angled forwards and to the left because the blowhole is positioned to the left and forwards. Toothed whales have a single blowhole and baleen whales have two. Blows soon after emerging from a dive usually show a bigger column of water vapour. Time spent on the surface and the number of blows vary from one species to another. Many whale species usually remain stationary on the surface when they have come up from a feeding dive. Dolphins are constantly on the move.

Above: *A female Sperm Whale performs a belly roll. The purpose of this behaviour is unknown.*

Below left and right: *The different profiles of the blows. A Blue Whale's blow (left) is tall and vertical. A Sperm Whale's (right) is low and bushy, forward pointing and slanted to the left.*

Breaching and lunging During breaching a substantial part of a whale's body leaves the water. A 'lunge' occurs when only a small part of the body leaves the water. Most people would assume that a breaching whale is a male showing off to females. However, Hal Whitehead, in his classic book *Sperm Whales: Social Evolution in the Ocean*, pointed out that male Sperm Whales do not breach as part of courtship behaviour. He also noted that breaching and spy hopping by female Sperm Whales increased in the presence of visiting males.

Above: An adult female Sperm Whale breaches, possibly as a response to the presence of a visiting adult male.

Below: A Blue Whale side-flukes.

Bow riding Dolphins in particular will ride the bow wave of a boat. When this occurs, it is important for a boat to avoid suddenly changing speed or direction to avoid injuring the dolphins. Many dolphin species bow ride by travelling in the pressure wave created in front of a travelling vessel. In Sri Lanka Spinner Dolphins often bow ride in front of whale-watching and fishing boats. At the same time other individuals may spin.

Cetacean wave Certain species of cetacean are often found travelling and feeding together. I have adapted the popular term 'bird wave' to describe this phenomenon as a 'cetacean wave', because the benefits of different species associating together in groups must be similar, providing added security and increased foraging efficiency, for example. Commonly seen cetacean waves in Sri Lanka comprise Short-finned Pilot Whales and Bottlenose Dolphins. These species do not, however, seem to form stable associations, unlike those of the Sinharaja bird waves described earlier, although this could be a perception caused by limited opportunity to observe cetacean behaviour.

Chorus line When hunting for food, cetaceans such as Sperm Whales foraging off the Kalpitiya Peninsula may arrange themselves along parallel lines, forming waves of animals stretched across several miles.

Right: The box-like head of a Sperm Whale slices through the water. The viscous Spermaceti may act as a buoyancy control, an acoustic lens or both.

Spinner Dolphins off Mirissa, Trincomalee and Kalpitiya are often seen forming chorus lines that may consist of 5–10 individuals abreast, with many such 'wavelets' being formed by hundreds or even a thousand plus dolphins.

Courtship The courtship of the great baleen whales is known from species such as the Humpback Whale, where males may engage in aggressive chases of a female. Courthship movements have been seen to involve flank formations with the female believed to lead the pair.

Deep dive A deep dive is usually signalled by a whale lifting its tail flukes clear out of the water. Deep dives are usually for feeding, but whales dive deeply if a fast-moving boat approaches them closely. Blue Whales typically feed in the top 60 m (200 ft), but may descend to 400 m (1,300 ft). Sperm Whales typically feed at around 400 m (1,300 ft), but have been recorded as diving to depths of more than 2 km (1¼ miles). On several occasions I have seen Sperm Whales deep diving off the Kalpitiya Peninsula in the Sperm Whale line, which is 400 m (1,300 ft) in depth. I have also encountered Sperm Whales that had defecated after feeding off Trincomalee, where the depth was between 2 and 3 km (1¼ and 1¾ miles).

Elephants of the sea Sperm Whales are highly intelligent, social animals. They are the elephants of the sea, with complex social structures. They communicate by using clicks that form dialects, which are sometimes specific to groups. The only animals more curious than Leopard cubs seem to me to be Sperm Whales. My three best encounters with Sperm Whales have all been when I have been with children on a small boat. I have wondered whether these highly intelligent animals feel that they are less at risk from a boat that has children on it. Perhaps some of them are old enough to remember that the whaling boats that hunted them did not have children on board? Or maybe they are just more curious about boats containing mixed-age pods of humans? I have, however, also observed Sperm Whales almost nudge boats that had only adults on board, so though child-friendly Sperm Whales have the makings of a nice story, it may in fact not be true. Perhaps these intelligent and curious animals simply know that boats in Sri Lankan waters do not represent any danger to them. If Sperm Whale watching is handled responsibly from small boats in Kalpitiya, it will be wonderful to one day see Sperm Whales coming to interact closely with boats, as do the renowned Grey Whales (*Eschrichtius robustus*) in Baja California, which come up to boats for people to scratch them.

Flipper slapping and waving Some species of whale, notably the Humpback Whale, can turn on their side and bring up a flipper into the air to wave or to slap the water. This is probably a form of social behaviour, with the slaps on the water sending an acoustic message. It is almost never seen off Sri Lankan waters, although I did once obtain distant views of two suspected Blue Whales that breached and also flipper waved.

Head raising Sperm Whales often swim up to a boat and lift up their heads in what I call a 'head raise'. In a head raise the body remains horizontal, unlike in spy hopping, where the body is in a vertical position. The eyes are not above the water in this posture, and I am not sure if there is a visual benefit in this position. Perhaps it is used to fire an echolocating beam of sonar through the air to better profile the boat and its occupants? Can the animals gauge the number, ages and sizes of the occupants?

Head-stand and fluking Whales may lift their tails out of the water and hold them suspended aloft in what is described as a head-stand (or tail extension in some North American literature). Some authors describe this behaviour as a tail stand. This is very different behaviour from fluking, which involves bringing the tail flukes momentarily above the water in a fairly smooth and continuous movement before submerging for a deep dive.

When it comes to the European term fluking, described by North Americans as fluke up, in a still picture it may be difficult to distinguish between a head-stand and fluking. In the former, a cetacean may lift the tail stock more out of the water than it would do in fluking.

Fluke print Fluke prints are easily observed when Blue Whales dive. They are clear patches of water that remain on the surface.

Jaw clapping Sperm Whales are known to lift their heads out of the water and clap their jaws, showing their teeth. The purpose of this behaviour is not clear. It could be a part of social interaction with other whales or aggression towards them. I once saw a Sperm Whale jaw clapping during a period of active socialization by a pod of Sperm Whales. This suggests that this is a form of social behaviour and may not necessarily involve aggression.

Left: A Sperm Whale begins a deep-feeding dive. Despite its size, it is likely to be an adult female from a 'breeding school' in the tropics, rather than a visiting bull male from high latitudes.

Lob-tailing (tail slapping) Both whales and dolphins slap the water for what is believed to be a number of reasons, varying from aggression and excitement to stunning prey. Tail slapping by large whales is referred to as lob-tailing. Large whales have been observed to give several slaps when lob-tailing.

Logging (or rafting) Sperm Whales are often seen in groups floating like logs on the water. This rest position is called logging or rafting. Logging is defined as a position in which the whales do not show forwards movement. When travelling their bodies appear on the surface in a similar way, except that they have a strong directional movement.

Lunge feeding Baleen whales explosively break the surface of the water as they rise up with their jaws open to scoop up fish. This behaviour is most famously associated with Humpback Whales. I have seen a Blue Whale break the surface of the water with its head slightly above the water, and it may well have been scooping up krill at the surface. However, this is not lunge feeding, which is unlikely to be seen in Sri Lankan waters given the scarcity of Humpback Whales in this location.

Porpoising (running) Porpoising or running usually occurs when a dolphin is travelling at speed and repeatedly exposes its body in little jumps out of the water. With each jump it arcs its body and re-enters the water cleanly, head first. Porpoising may allow the animal to travel at greater speed than it would by swimming through water alone, as air is less resistant than water, although more energy may be expended in the series of small jumps. Dolphins porpoise, but porpoises do not.

Roll-over A roll-over occurs when a whale rotates through 360 degrees, bringing the pectoral fins (side flippers) into view. Roll-overs by Blue and Sperm Whales occur in Sri Lankan waters, but are rare.

Rooster tail A cetacean travelling at speed near the surface of the water can create two outwards-spreading curtains of water. Viewed from a side, these create an impression of a rooster's tail.

Rushing (skidding) At times cetaceans rush through the water then break speed, rather like a vehicle that has hit a wet patch, applied the brakes and skidded. This is clearly some form of social behaviour. In large pods of more than 500 Spinner Dolphins, I have sometimes seen a few dolphins engaging in rushing. This could be a way of demonstrating their fitness and establishing a dominance hierarchy. Some people think the animals are just having fun.

Scrumming and active socializing The term 'scrumming' is used here in the absence of established terminology to describe a form of active socializing by Sperm Whales. On one whale-watching trip off Trincomalee, I saw that for a couple of minutes the water near the boat turned to a frothing mass as four or five Sperm Whales rushed into each other and writhed in the water as though they were in a rugby scrum. Was this a bunch of females and immatures rushing to greet a male, or females and young interacting in what is described as active socializing? I suspect it was a form of social bonding between females and immatures.

Above and centre: *Sperm Whale family pods can engage in scrumming, during which they rush into each other and are very physical with a lot of contact as in a rugby scrum. A tail-fluke sticks out during a scrum (centre) and another whale makes a fast belly-roll (above).*

Opposite left, above and below: *Lob-tailing can be a sign of aggression or a signal. This was probably females signalling to each other.*

Sexual dimorphism Some whales, such as Sperm Whales, show what scientists call sexual dimorphism, which is a way of saying that the sexes look physically different. A mature bull Sperm Whale can be a third bigger than a female and weigh twice as much, and his dorsal fin is more towards the back than that of a female. Size is very hard to gauge in the field, unless a whale is close to a boat so that the length of the boat can be used as a reference. A further complication is that many whales only show a limited section of their length at any given time. In some cetacean species the presence of scarring on the heads and bodies marks out mature males, which show the scars of old battles. In Short-finned Pilot Whales mature males can be identified by their large dorsal fins, which are broad based and flag shaped. In the young and females they are more falcate.

Side-fluking (side-sharking) This is where the triangular tip of a tail fluke is raised above the water and dragged along. The description 'side-sharking' or 'shark-fin patrolling' may convey a better image. The term 'side-fluking' used by researchers such as Hal Whitehead gives a more static impression of a tail fluke merely sticking out of the water sideways. At Trincomalee I have seen side-fluking or side-sharking in Sperm Whales that have socialized close by. On two occasions the whales did this so close to the boat that it felt like a scene from *Jaws*, with a shark stalking the boat. In April 2012 I photographed a Blue Whale side-fluking off Mirissa, though this behaviour is rarely noted in Blue Whales.

Sharking This occurs when a cetacean shows just the exposed tip of its dorsal fin as it travels along, presenting a classic shark profile. Dolphins do this very often with nothing but the dorsal fin showing. This may perhaps happen when they are asleep and not very active.

Skimming This is unique to Rough-toothed Dolphins, which are rarely seen in Sri Lankan waters. In this behaviour, a dolphin swims fast with its head and chin (and hence beak) out of the water.

Sleeping and resting It may seem odd to mention this in an account of cetacean surface behaviour. However, this is an activity that many observers see without realizing that they have done so. Cetaceans, being mammals, have to breathe air otherwise they will drown. They therefore have to surface to breathe and be active, but they also need to sleep. They have

Left: Sperm Whales engage in shark-fin patrolling – a side-fluking display in which one tail fluke is dragged relatively slowly over the water, then dragged in. From left to right, the first two pictures show a front view, the third a side view.

dealt with these conflicting needs by developing the ability to switch off one side of the brain at a time. Thus even when they are sleeping they will be travelling very slowly or milling around near the surface to breathe. Many dolphins seen during the day, especially those that are seemingly sluggish in their behaviour, are sleeping. Many of the dolphins seen inshore of the reef off the Kalpitiya Peninsula are sleeping or resting; they go offshore of the reef into deeper water to hunt during the night.

Spinning Spinner Dolphins are regularly seen hurling themselves into the air and spinning around their longitudinal axis. There are a number of theories as to why they do this. One is that it is a sign of their fitness and that males are displaying to females. Alternatively, this may simply be a form of social behaviour practised by both sexes. An extension of this view is that the loud splashes may be a signal for other dolphins to gather for social behaviour or feeding. Spinning seems to occur only in large pods, and it is possible that it may have a social function. A more practical reason for it may be that the 4 g-force generated on spins forces parasites such as remoras (Echeneidae spp.) to let go. Spinner Dolphins usually have no remoras attached to them, and spinning may indeed serve a practical purpose. Another view is that the dolphins are simply engaging in the behaviour for fun. This is possible as cetaceans are highly intelligent and may have a range of emotions similar to our own.

Splash guard The blowhole of a whale is closed by special valves to prevent water from entering the lungs. Some of the large baleen whales, such as the Blue Whale, show a pronounced splash guard around the blowhole. The raised enclosure around the blowhole may offer further protection from water dribbling in.

Spy hopping This is when a whale brings its body into a vertical position with its head out of the water. It is thought that this allows whales to have a better view of what is on the surface; for example, Orcas may scan for seals on ice floes in this way. Although Sperm Whales have regularly swum up to my boat and raised their heads, I have rarely seen them spy hopping. Once I counted seven Sperm Whales taking it in turn to spy hop. Either the spy hopping was part of a behavioural ritual, or they wanted to look at us more critically. Hal Whitehead has noted that spy hopping seems to increase when mature male Sperm Whales visit pods of females and subadults.

Super-pods Whales and dolphins are sociable animals that live in pods or groups of varying sizes. When different pods come together for feeding or other reasons, super-pods form. Sperm Whales are typically found in pods of less than 25 individuals. Spinner Dolphins can be seen in pods of around seven individuals, and pods of 500 are not rare. In Kalpitiya the term super-pod for Spinner Dolphins is used when the numbers are in the order of 2,000 individuals.

Surface sequence Many whales engage in a distinctive sequence when they surface or dive, showing different parts of their bodies at different stages. Most whales on the water's surface show the area around the blowhole as they surface and blow, followed by the dorsal fin coming up. A Sei Whale, on the other hand, rises up like a submarine, with the blowhole and dorsal fin surfacing simultaneously. Blue Whales rarely show the fronts of their heads, while Sperm Whales travelling on the water's surface clearly show the bulbous fronts of their heads. Most whales show their dorsal fin when resting and breathing. When a whale begins a dive, its body begins to roll like a 'wheel', with the dorsal fin going under and the tail stock being raised or arched. On a deep dive the larger whales raise their tail flukes out of the water and fluke up. At times they may roll and slip into the water without showing their tail flukes. As already mentioned (see page 120), whales should not be pursued to take the classic tail-fluke shot. Sometimes whales swim up to a boat and turn away and fluke-up, providing an opportunity for photography without stressing the animals.

Trumpeting Also known as bubbling, this is a type of behaviour in which a whale blows up a fountainhead of water. It's not clear if this is the intended action or whether it's a by-product of some other action. It has

also been observed in Blue Whales in Baja California and seems to be part of their courtship repertoire.

Vocalizations, echolocation and sound There are accounts of people being able to hear the sonar pulses of Sperm Whales fired into the air close to boats. Whalers in wooden ships used to hear the pulses bouncing off their wooden hulls and called Sperm Whales 'carpenter fish', because the pulses sounded like nails being driven into wood. Toothed whales use sound pulses to hunt in the same way as do echolocating bats. Baleen whales use long waves to communicate. Blue Whales are believed to be able to communicate over a few thousand kilometres. Our normal understanding of a group does not hold with cetaceans as they can be in close social contact but not physically within sight of each other.

The increasing levels of noise in the sea pose a huge challenge to these animals, which have evolved to communicate across great distances, but can no longer do so because of the background sound levels. When whale watching, cutting off the boat engine produces the best results, increasing the possibility of whales becoming inquisitive and approaching the boat.

Wake riding Some dolphin species like to ride the wakes of boats. Spinner Dolphins are sometimes seen doing this. The Striped Dolphins occasionally seen in Sri Lankan waters are also known to wake ride.

Above: *A Blue Whale trumpets or bubbles a fountainhead of water during an unusual courtship display off Mirissa. The function of this display is unknown and the trumpeting may primarily be an acoustic display.*

Opposite: *A Spinner Dolphin spins into the air before crashing into the water in a display which can be seen from over a kilometre away. The sound generated may serve as a social signal.*

Whale Watching in Mirissa

6 January

A knock on my door at 6 a.m. at the Sanmira Renaissance in Una Watuna. I open the door to find one of the staff with a tray bearing a pot of tea. I am sure the boat crew enjoyed the packed breakfast I gave them. Hotels all along the coastline were full. I was at the Mirissa harbour by 6.30, to board the *Spirit of Dondra* for a private booking by Shyamalee Tudawe, the editor of *Hi Magazine*. Some more of my friends were sailing on the larger *Jayasayura*. I joined them on the top deck and gave a short talk of about 15 minutes with the help of the two admirality charts I had. The charts showed the depth isobars around Sri Lanka and in the south. I rejoined the *Spirit of Dondra*.

We saw a few seabirds. The most interesting were some five Bridled Terns about 10 km (5 nautical miles) due south from Mirissa. At the harbour I had seen Great Crested and Little Terns. A few Barn Swallows (*Hirundo rustica*) were visible over the sea at distances of between 10 and 20 km (5 and 10 nautical miles). A Crimson Rose (*Pachliopta hector*) butterfly was also encountered at around 35 km (19 nautical miles) out.

When we were about 20 km (10 nautical miles) out, I joined the crew to scan from the top deck for Blue Whales. At 9.55 we saw the first Blue Whale spout. Soon another was seen, then another. There were at least three Blue Whales in our sights.

The crew are now quite good at handling Blue Whales. They will not make a direct bearing to an animal and scare it. Instead they approach parallel to it and at a distance, so that it is comfortable with the boat. As a result we never got very close to Blue Whales, except when they chose to surface near the boat. We watched for more than an hour, and the Blue Whales never felt pursued by the boat. At one time we made out that there were at least five unique animals in our field of view. They were not all spouting simultaneously, but the spouts occurred a few minutes apart and from different angles, showing that at least five individuals were present. They included a mother and calf – we made sure we kept a fair distance from them.

On two occasions Blue Whales (possibly the same individual) turned and swam towards the boat, showing curiosity. They fluked rarely, most of the time slipping into the water to feed, having spent a few minutes at the surface to exhale. One Blue Whale surfaced about 7 m (23 ft) away from the boat. Nedra Hewavitharana, who saw it emerge, was so speechless that several people partially missed it until Shyamalee, who was facing towards the back, yelled out.

At one time there were four whale-watching boats fanning out over 2 km (1¼ miles) across the ocean, drawing an invisible net to trawl for Blue Whales. When the encounters began, all four boats kept to their own cluster of sightings. It could have been the same five individuals, spaced a few kilometres apart, that were surfacing around the four boats, or possibly there may have been anything up to ten in the area. Even if one takes the most conservative estimate, this was a phenomenal encounter, like that of several by the whale-watching boats in the last two weeks. I am increasingly convinced that the hypothesis by Dr Anderson, which predicts a peak in the eastwards movement between December and January, must be right. This does not mean that there cannot be a sedentary population year round.

As I drove back to Colombo, Angelo Samarawickrama, who was on the *Jayasayura*, texted me to say that they had also had an amazing encounter with a Blue Whale that had surfaced right next to the boat.

The Blue Whales in our waters are used to heavy marine traffic on the shipping lanes, and to fishing vessels. If, as on this day, the whale-watching boats simply mill around in the water without pursuing the whales for a close look, the animals will swim up to the boats or surface very close to them. At times on this occasion, naked-eye views were close enough to show the remoras clinging to the backs of the whales.

Clockwise from below left: *Crimson Roses mating; a Bridled Tern in worn plumage; a Blue Whale with remoras attached to it.*

Right: *Bryde's Whales are tropical species which can surface and sink unobtrusively.*

Mini Field Guide: Cetaceans and Seabirds

Despite the large number of boats now taking people out to whale watch in Sri Lanka, there is still a surprising absence of fieldcraft skills to identify some of the marine mammals and rarely seen seabirds that are encountered. Below is a mini field guide for whale watchers. I have included here the most common cetaceans that visitors are likely to be able to identify, as well as the striking Whale Shark (a fish). Pelagic seabirds that were once considered great rarities are now increasingly seen on whale-watching trips, and in this section I also draw attention to them.

Cetaceans

Blue Whale 25 m (82 ft). Usually solitary or a mother and calf. Skin is smooth. Close views show mottling on a blue-grey background. Dorsal fin is tiny, at times like a little hook. Blow is tall and vertical. When feeding, surfaces every 10–12 minutes. The geographical race of the Blue Whale found off Sri Lankan waters is shorter than that found in higher latitudes (the Atlantic, North Pacific and Antarctic).

Bryde's Whale 16.5 m (54 ft) female, 15 m (49 ft) male. Occasionally seen. Much smaller than the Blue Whale, with a less powerful vertical blow. Dorsal fin is curved back and 'pointy'. Very different from the short, stubby dorsal fin of the Blue Whale. Unusually, females are longer than males.

Sperm Whale 12 m (39 ft) female, 18.3 m (60 ft) male. Often seen in pods of 7–10. Occasionally super-pods form. Skin is wrinkly like a wet sock that has been squeezed to dry out. Dorsal fin is clear and rounded. Blow is short and bushy. At close quarters it can be seen to be pointing forwards and to the left. Tail flukes are narrower than the Blue Whale's and triangular in shape. Males are a third longer than females. Most Sperm Whales in pods seen off Sri Lanka are females and young males.

Short-finned Pilot Whale 1.4–1.9 m (4½–6¼ ft). Very dark, looking black at times. Chunky bodied with a bulbous head, bigger than the Spinner Dolphin's. Dorsal fin has a broad base and curves back. In older males the fin is very large and blunt, almost flag shaped. Always in small pods. Often in the company of Bottlenose Dolphins.

Indo-Pacific Humpback Dolphin 2.6–2.8 m (8½–9 ft). Grey and pink with a distinctive wide base to the dorsal fin, which gives rise to the 'humped back'. Mature adults show a lot of pink, especially on the tail and belly. Requires a focused search in the Puttalam Lagoon, usually accessed from the Kalpitiya Peninsula, with an encounter rate of about one in three trips. Seems very rare, and recent records are only from Kalpitiya. The dolphins seen around Sri Lanka are the 'plumbea' type, and have more grey and less pink than the ones further east.

Bottlenose dolphin 1.9–3.8 m (6¼–12½ ft). Uniformly grey with a blunt tip – the 'bottle-nose'. Seen regularly close to Mirissa Harbour. Probably overlooked as it is much less acrobatic than the Spinner Dolphin. Has been split into two species: Common Bottlenose Dolphin (*Tursiops truncatus*) and Indo-Pacific Bottlenose Dolphin (*T. aduncus*). The latter is characterized by spotting in the ventral area. Work needs to be done to ascertain which species, or whether both species, are found off Sri Lanka.

Spinner Dolphin 2.0–2.35 m (6½–7¾ ft). Long snouted; the only species in Sri Lanka to spin, although other species may leap out of the water. Usually in large pods. Those off Sri Lanka are a subspecies known as Gray's Spinner Dolphin. Three tone in colour with a dark cape, lighter sides and pale belly. The belly cannot be seen from the surface, so the animals appear two-toned.

Pantropical Spotted Dolphin 1.6–2.6 m (5¼–8½ ft). Likes to bow ride. Occasionally leaps out of the water. Tip of beak has a pale spot. Dark cape on top of light body. Appears two toned on the surface, like the Spinner Dolphin. Look for absence of eye-to-anus stripe in Pantropical Spotted. Also lacks eye-to-flipper stripe and instead has a lower jaw-to-flipper stripe. Shape of the pale area on this species gives it an obvious 'pale face' compared with that of the Spinner Dolphin. Pantropical Spotted Dolphins seen around Sri Lanka are of the offshore variety that has hardly any spots on top.

Striped Dolphin 2.5 m (8¼ ft). Can be acrobatic, often leaping high into the air. Two clear stripes lead from eye to flipper and anus. Both stripes contrast strongly with the pale sides. Eye-to-anus stripe has another short, thin line that breaks out near the eye.

Above: An Indo-Pacific Humpback Dolphin (or Pink Dolphin) tail slaps in the Puttalam Lagoon.

Left: The dorsal fins of Short-finned Pilot Whales become increasingly flag-shaped with age.

Right: A Whale Shark, the largest fish in the world, about to nudge our boat.

Opposite: Some Brown Noddies show a little white on the forehead.

Fish

Whale Shark 8–14 m (26¼–46 ft). The largest fish in the world. Neither a marine mammal nor a shark. Seen off both Mirissa and Trincomalee. Inquisitive and docile. Large size, patterns of spots on the body and blunt head are distinctive. Dorsal fin often mistaken for a shark's fin.

Birds

There are several good guide books for Sri Lankan birds, so this section is restricted to a few species that were rarely seen until whale watching provided access to pelagic seabirds. The best time to see these birds is just before the onset of the south-west monsoon, from the end of March to the first two weeks of April. When the seas become too rough, shore-based watching may yield pelagic seabirds that are blown in under stormy conditions. Whale watching off Trincomalee and Mirissa has given access to rarely seen pelagic seabirds, but my favourite site is the Kalpitiya Peninsula (see page 112), which is now recognized as an Asian hotspot for pelagics.

Flesh-footed Shearwater 41–45 cm (16–17¾ in). Tail shorter and more rounded than that of the Wedge-tailed Shearwater. Legs and feet pink, but not diagnostic as shared with Wedge-tailed. Stout pink bill with dark tip is the best field characteristic. In flight in good light, primaries show a pale patch.

Wedge-tailed Shearwater 41–46 cm (16–18 in). Flesh-coloured feet like the Flesh-footed Shearwater. More slender, all-dark bill best separates it from

Flesh-footed. Wedge tail does not always show well. Bill pattern is the best field characteristic. Longer necked than Flesh-footed, but this is not always apparent.

Persian Shearwater 30.5–33 cm (12–13 in). Pale underparts, brown upperparts. Bill grey with a darker tip. On two occasions in April 2011, I came across Persian Shearwaters in mixed seabird flocks that contained only one or two Persian Shearwaters. By contrast, earlier in April 2010 I located one flock that contained 35 Persian Shearwaters. I am sure that as increasing numbers of birdwatchers hire boats to run north–south transects between the E 79 35 and E 79 38 lines of longitude, many hitherto scarcely seen pelagics will be seen and photographed.

Long-tailed Skua 35–41 cm (13½–16 in) (excluding tail streamers). Long tail streamers are distinctive. One I saw on the sea off Kalpitiya reminded me of a Pheasant-tailed Jacana (*Hydrophasianus chirurgus*).

Pomarine Skua 56 cm (22 in). Typical adult has twisted tail tips, giving a rounded blunt tip. More pot-bellied than the Arctic Skua. On sailings from Mirissa I have seen flocks of up to 20 birds, although single birds are more likely to be seen. I have photographed Pomarines off Kalpitiya, but they are rarely seen there.

General note on skuas: these birds can be difficult to identify unless they are adults with the tail showing the typical pattern, without any damage or wear distorting its shape. Advanced guides need to be consulted to identify immatures. Skuas are seen as the south-west monsoon approaches.

Lesser Noddy 32 cm (12½ in). Smaller than the Brown Noddy, with a fine, long bill. Greyish lores contrast with dark smudge around the eye. Lores can often look white and in some birds extend to the crown, nape and upper back. Under-wing uniformly brown, lacking contrast of Brown Noddy's. Wingbeats quicker than in Brown Noddy.

Brown Noddy 42 cm (16½ in). Pale bar across upper-wing coverts contrasts with the flight feathers. Under-wing coverts paler and contrast with the dark flight feathers, but this is not apparent unless lighting conditions permit it. Chocolate-brown tail contrasts with the paler back. Pale forehead extends to the crown; can be very white in some birds. Lores dark, looking black. Beak more down-curved than Lesser Noddy's. Bill heavy and jagged compared with Lesser Noddy's. Wing flaps in flight distinctly slower and more laboured than those of Lesser Noddy. Tail bigger and more spoon shaped than Lesser Noddy's. Also has a habit of bringing the tail down at right angles to the body when it needs to break air speed.

Sooty Tern 33–36 cm (13–14 in). Blacker upperparts than Bridled Tern's. White forehead does not extend over the eye. Black and white tail. Scarce; Kalpitiya seems to be one of the best places to see it, with reports of exhausted birds seen resting on beach.

Bridled Tern (Brown-winged Tern) 30–32 cm (11¾–12½ in). One of the most frequently seen seabirds on whale watches, but had been seen only by a tiny handful of shore-based birdwatchers before that. Brown upperparts and pale under-body. Under-wing coverts white with flight feathers brown. Tail brownish. Wing coverts and mantle slightly paler brown than primaries, but this is not obvious in the field. White extends over the eye, forming a short, but thick supercilium.

5
Sri Lanka's National Parks and Wildlife Reserves

Specific site descriptions are listed by habitat type to give a good idea of what a visitor can expect to see. The south has been a popular tourist destination since the 1980s, and wildlife tourists have begun to stop over here since 2008 for whale watching. What is not yet widely known is that it has a few good rainforests within easy reach of the port city of Galle as detailed in this chapter.

Left: *The Oriental Bay Owl* (Phodilus badius assimilis) *is an elusive and enigmatic forest owl. The bird in Sri Lanka could in future be split into an endemic species.*

Map of Sri Lanka's National Parks and Reserves

INDIA
Palk Strait
Bay of Bengal
Bay of Bengal
INDIAN OCEAN
Delft
Kayts
Palk Bay
Jaffna Lagoon
Devil's Point
Mannar
Adam's Bridge
Mannar Island
NORTHERN
Pigeon Island
Portugal Bay
Wilpattu National Park
Foul Point
NORTH CENTRAL
Gulf of Mannar
Puttalam Lagoon
Kaudulla National Park
Minneriya National Park
Elephant Point
NORTH WESTERN
Annaiwilundawa
Wasgomuwa National Park
Deduru Oya
EASTERN
Maduru Oya National Park
KNUCKLES RANGE
Kandy Lake
Gal Oya National Park
WESTERN
CENTRAL
Kithulgala (Kelani Valley) Rainforest
UVA
Bodhinagala
Adam's Peak
2243m
Horton Plains National Park
Talangama Wetland
Yala (Ruhuna) National Park
Uda Walawe National Park
Sinharaja Rainforest
Little Basses
Kanneliya Forest Reserve
Great Basses
SOUTHERN
Bundala National Park
Kottawa Rainforest and Arboretum
Kalametiya Sanctuary
Hiyare Rainforest Park
Dondra Head
N
0
50 km
0
50 miles

Monsoon Rains

A key factor that needs to be taken into account when visiting sites in Sri Lanka is the monsoon rains. The south-west monsoon is from May to August and the north-east monsoon is from October to January. The monsoon months may be wet, limiting the hours spent in the field. Furthermore, the inter-monsoonal period in October can at times bring more rain than the monsoons to the wet zone in the south-west quadrant of the island. However, the rainy season has its own rewards and the sites are productive year round for viewing natural history. Do bear in mind that during the north-east monsoon access is not possible to Minneriya and Kaudulla National Parks. Road access to the wet-zone lowland rainforests may sometimes be difficult, with the main roads to them closed for a day or so due to flooding. Whale watching is not possible during the prevailing monsoon on the west or east coasts. The mountains receive rain from both monsoons, but mainly from the south-west monsoon.

SITE	BEST TIME OF YEAR	MONSOON*
Talangama	November to April benefits from migrant birds.	South-west (May–August).
Annaiwilundawa	As above.	
Bundala	As above.	
Kalametiya	As above.	
Wilpattu	As above. Leopards all year. Sloth Bear best in June and July.	North-east (October–January).
Wasgomuwa	Elephants all year.	North-east (October–January).
Minneriya (and Kaudulla)	Elephants June to September. No access during monsoon.	North-east (October–January. Monsoon limits access.
Yala	Leopards, elephants and Sloth Bear all year. Sloth Bear best in June and July.	North-east (October–January). Monsoon does not adversely impact game drives although rain is experienced.
Uda Walawe	Elephants guaranteed all year.	South-west (May–August). Monsoon reduces access to parts of the park.
Horton Plains	Endemic birds and other animals all year.	South-west (May–August). Expect mist and fog.
Bodhinagala	As above.	South-west (May–August).
Sinharaja	Endemic birds and other animals all year.	South-west (May–August).
Kithulgala	As above.	South-west (May–August). During heavy rain, access via a bridge instead of the usual ferry.
Rainforests of Galle (Kottawa, Hiyare and Kanneliya)	As above.	South-west (May–August). Expect times where an entire day is heavily overcast.
Maduru Oya	Elephants year round.	North-east (October–January).
Gal Oya	Elephants year round.	North-east (October–January).
Knuckles	Endemic birds and other animals all year.	South-west (May–August).

*Mentioned if it is a pronounced factor

Wetlands

Talangama Wetland

This wetland on the outskirts of Colombo is bordered by motorable roads, which make access easy for wildlife enthusiasts. The complex of ponds, canals and paddy fields makes it a rich and varied wetland site. Colombo as a capital is blessed to have such a suburban jewel.

Wildlife More than a hundred bird species have been recorded here. In one morning during winter, I recorded 70 species. Birding highlights are the migrant Black and Yellow Bitterns (*Dupetor flavicollis flavicollis* and *Ixobrychus sinensis*), which supplement the local population, and the Watercock (*Gallicrex cinerea cinerea*). The mammals list is surprisingly rich, with a very good chance of encountering the endemic Purple-faced Leaf Monkey. Other mammals found here include the Ruddy Mongoose (*Herpestes smithii*), endemic Yellow-striped Chevrotain (*Moschiola kathygre*), Black-naped Hare, Fishing Cat and Crested Porcupine. However, due to predation by dogs and threats from humans, many of these animals have become nocturnal and are at risk as their forest cover continues to be lost to housing development. Talangama is also good for the most common butterflies and dragonflies. More than 30 dragonfly species are found here.

Getting there Get to Wewa Para (Lake Road) via Akuregoda Road or Wickramasinghapura Road, both of which are off the Pannipitiya Road, a few kilometres from the Parliament. Free access on public roads.

Accommodation Villa Talangama overlooks one of the best stretches of wetland. City hotels in Colombo are only 30–45 minutes away.

***Right:** Black-headed Ibis (*Threskiornis melanocephalus*) and Asian Openbills (*Anastomus oscitans*) feed in Talangama Wetland.*

Dragonflies and Fighting Swamphens in Talangama

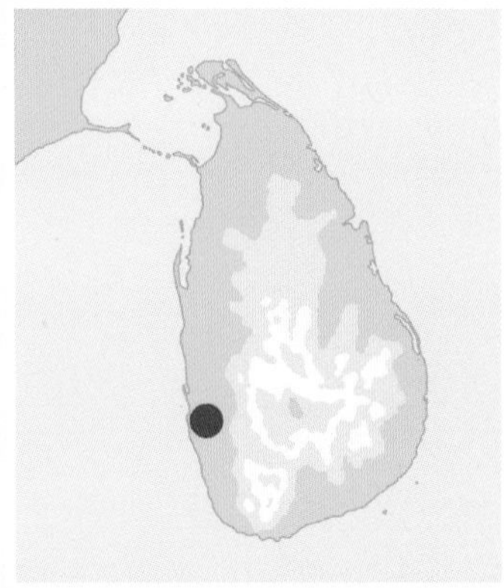

15 March

Arrived at about 8 a.m. and went to the marshes beyond Villa Talangama. Two Painted Storks (*Mycteria leucocephala*) were feeding close to each other. Their feeding technique involved inserting the bill into the mud through the vegetation and water, and shaking the area with one foot. The birds allowed a close approach as they were used to people. A Little Cormorant (*Phalacrocorax niger*) showed some white on the throat.

At about 9 a.m. I photographed fighting Purple Swamphens (*Porphyrio porphyrio poliocephalus*) for about 45 minutes. One bird in particular seemed to initiate many of the fights. It looked to be the biggest, but this could be because of how it had fluffed up its feathers. Perhaps it had gained dominance during the latter stages of the fighting as many birds chose to run away when it approached them. The behaviour seemed to point to an alpha male structure, where the dominant male secures access to the majority of the females.

Left: *A Little Cormorant vibrates its throat, possibly as a way of losing heat.*

Opposite, clockwise from above: *Purple Swamphens clash; a Purple Heron; a Common Kingfisher (*Alcedo atthis*) – a male, identified by its all-black beak.*

The two Purple Swamphens grappled each other and lay on the ground for at least 15 minutes. Each would wrap its long toes around the neck, head or both of the other at various times. At times one or two other birds would approach but did not join in the fight. Occasionally the two would lose their grip on each other and erupt into the air, flailing at each other with their legs. I lost sight of them after a while. Later I saw what could have been one of the birds, which had been immersed in water, coming out. I am not sure if its opponent had been drowned as a result of the half an hour's combat. Another bird approached the bedraggled one and on at least three occasions stretched its toes wide and placed them on the back of the wet bird and pushed away. It seemed to realize that the bedraggled bird could not put up a fight and that simply pushing it away with a foot would be enough to establish the pecking order. Once I saw two birds flying into the air and flailing their legs at each other. After they landed another bird engaged in aerial combat with one of the pair. Generally a pair of birds would fight until one ran away. Apart from on this occasion, I did not see a fight being interrupted by another bird entering the fray. One bird gave a broken-wing display and stayed at the edges. If it was chased by another it ran away, whereupon the other potential combatants seemed to give up the chase easily. Perhaps it was clearly signalling that it was not ready to fight with the broken-wing display.

I flushed a Yellow Bittern, Barn Swallows and a Yellow Wagtail (*Motacilla flava*). A juvenile female Black-winged Stilt (*Himantopus himantopus himantopus*) seen on the last visit was still present.

I then moved to the privately owned 'One Acre' reserve, where I saw a Common Iora (*Aegithina tiphia multicolor*) and heard an Oriental Honey-buzzard (*Pernis ptilorhynchus orientalis*), Dark-fronted Babbler, White-browed Bulbul (*Pycnonotus luteolus insulae*) and other birds.

At around 12 noon a male Purple-faced Leaf Monkey vocalized very strongly and aggressively for a minute or so. The leaf monkeys were also raiding a Jak tree.

A medium-sized Water Monitor entered the water from the island. Later, as I left at around 12.15, a Land Monitor walked outside the lower gate. I also saw adult Green Garden and Common Garden Lizards. A Bronze-backed Tree-snake (*Dendrelaphis tristis*) sped away. This species seems to be very shy.

Several butterflies were in the air, but the Yamfly I had seen recently was absent. There was a Banded Blue Pierrot on the wing. A Common Mime (*Chilasa clytia lankeswara*) was mud sipping and I could photograph it well.

I could clearly see at least two Sapphire Flutterers (*Rhyothemis triangularis*). The dragonfly species recorded in the One Acre include the following: Common Bluetail (*Ishnura senegalensis*), Painted Waxtail, Yellow Waxtail, Sprite (*Pseudagrion* sp.), Sri Lanka Orange-faced Sprite, Rapacious Flangetail (*Ictinogomphus rapax*), Oriental Scarlet, Blue Percher, Pied Parasol, Spine-legged Redbolt (*Rhodothemis rufa*), Sapphire Flutterer, Variable Flutterer, Elusive Adjutant and Scarlet Basker.

Close to 30 of the 37 species of dragonfly and damselfly recorded in the Talangama Wetland have been recorded in the 'One Acre' reserve.

Left: *A Common Bluetail (*Ischnura senegalensis*).*

Opposite, top row, left to right: *Purple-faced Leaf Monkey;* Argiope *sp. spider;* **middle row, left to right:** Euchromia polymena; *mating Indian Cupids (*Everes lacturnus*); Sapphire Flutterer;* **bottom row:** *Water Monitor.*

Annaiwilundawa

Annaiwilundawa refers to a cluster of freshwater tanks (including the Annaiwilundawa tank) that were collectively declared a sanctuary in 1997. The second Ramsar Site in Sri Lanka, this is one of the finest wetlands on the island for waterbirds.

Wildlife Waterfowl include the Little Grebe (*Tachybaptus ruficollis capensis*), Lesser Whistling-duck (*Dendocygna bicolor*) and Cotton Teal (*Nettapus coromandelianus*). Migrant birds include the Pintail (*Anas acuta acuta*), Garganey (*Anas querquedula*), and Common and Pintail Snipe (*Gallinago gallinago gallinago* and *G. stenura*). Large numbers of Asian Openbill and Little Cormorants nest here. Endemics include the Ceylon Wood-Shrike (*Tephrodornis affinis*) and Ceylon Swallow (*Hirundo hyperythra*). Mammals include the Grey Mongoose (*Herpestes edwardsi*). Following the north-east monsoon, the herbaceous edges are good for butterflies. Common and Plain Tigers, Lemon Pansy (*Junonia lemonias vaisya*), Joker, Crimson Rose, Common Sailor, Chocolate Soldier (*Junonia iphita pluviatalis*) and others can all be seen here.

Getting there At the 91 km post on the A3, 5 km (1/3 mile) past Arachchikattuwa town, is a turn-off to the left. Approximately 1.2 km (3/4 mile) down this road is the Suruwila tank on your left, and to your right is the main Annaiwilundawa tank.

Accommodation Negombo near the 31 km post on the A3 has a wide choice of accommodation. The Kalpitiya Peninsula has a smaller choice of a few resorts, many of them at the mid to high end.

Below: The first of the lakes in the Annaiwilundawa complex.

Opposite top: Annaiwilundawa and Talangama are two examples of outstanding wetlands for wildlife that are integrated into everyday living environments populated by people, roads and traffic.

Opposite below: A Tawny Coster, showing the 'beads' on the underwing.

Bundala National Park

Bundala National Park is a mix of scrub jungle and sand dunes bordering the sea. Its beaches are important nesting sites for turtles. The lagoons hold good numbers of birds and crocodiles.

Wildlife Endemic birds include the Brown-capped Babbler (*Pellorneum fuscocapillum*), Ceylon Wood-Shrike and Ceylon Junglefowl. During the northern winter large numbers of migrants arrive, such as Golden and Kentish Plovers (*Charadrius alexandrinus*), Large and Lesser Sand Plovers (*Charadrius leschenaultii* and *C. mongolus*), Marsh Sandpipers (*Tringa stagnatilis*) and Curlew Sandpipers, Curlew (*Numenius arquata orientalis*) and Greenshank. Rarities include the Broad-billed Sandpiper (*Limicola falcinellus falcinellus*) and Red-necked Phalarope.

The flora includes dry thorny scrub comprising the Andara (*Acacia leucophloea*), Kukurumana (*Catunaregam spinosa*), Eraminiya (*Ziziphus lucida*) and Karamba. The scrub-forest trees include the Maila (*Bauhinia racemosa*), Mustard Tree, Weera, Palu and Neem (*Azadirachta indica*). Mammals likely to be seen here include the Asian Elephant, Spotted Deer, Hanuman Langur, Golden Jackal, Black-naped Hare and Wild Pig (*Sus scrofa*). Olive Ridley and Leatherback Turtles and, more rarely, Hawksbill and Green Turtles, visit the beaches to lay eggs. This is also the best site for seeing Estuarine Crocodiles.

Getting there From the A2, at the Weligatta Junction near the 251 km post, take the turn to Bundala Village. The park office and entrance are on this road.

Accommodation Tissamaharama has a range of places to stay. Alternatively, there is accommodation close to Yala National Park.

Left: *Common Redshanks are common winter visitors.*

Opposite: *A lookout point at the Bundala National Park visitor centre.*

Below: *Bundala is a good place to see the Spot-billed Pelican (*Pelecanus philippensis*), which is internationally endangered.*

Kalametiya Sanctuary

Kalametiya is an extensive area of wetland with brackish lagoons, mangrove swamps, open grassy areas and pockets of scrub jungle. It is a key site for migrant waders, and provides an important refuge (one of the few remaining on the southern coastal strip) for the smaller mammals of Sri Lanka.

Wildlife Almost all the common wetland birds can be seen. Sought-after species include the Slaty-breasted Crake (*Gallirallus striatus albiventer*), Watercock and Black Bittern. During the northern winter the Glossy Ibis (*Plegadis falcinellus*) may be seen with thousands of waders. The Grey Mongoose and Hanuman Langur are the mammals most likely to be observed.

Getting there There are turn-offs to the sanctuary near to the 214 and 218 km posts on the A2 road near Hungama.

Accommodation There is good resort-type accommodation within an hour's drive of the sanctuary.

Mannar

Mannar Island and the strip on the mainland from around Giant's Tank have become magnets for birders in search of species that are not found regularly in the southern half of the island. These include Deccan avifaunal species such as the Long-tailed or Rufous-rumped Shrike (*Lanius schach caniceps*), Black Drongo (*Dicrurus macrocercus minor*), Crab Plover (*Dromas ardeola*) and Indian Courser (*Cursorius coromandelicus*). A few key sites in this area are described below.

Thalladi Pond Past the 80 km post, on the A14, a few hundred metres before the Mannar Causeway, on the right is a large freshwater pond. Star birds in Mannar, such as Spot-billed Ducks (*Anas poecilorhyncha*), often choose to occupy this pond, which is unfortunately beside a high-security zone.

Periyar Kalapuwa (lagoon) A finger of this lagoon crosses the A14, about 4 km ($2^1/_2$ miles) before the Mannar Causeway, near the 78 km post. Look for the Garganey, Common Teal (*Anas crecca crecca*) and Ringed Plover (*Charadrius hiaticula tundrae*). The seasonal wetland holds thousands of Wigeon (*Anas penelope*) and a few hundred Shovellers (*Anas clypeata*). The plains are also good for harriers (Circinae spp.).

Mannar Causeway The star birds here are the Oystercatcher (*Haematopus ostralegus longipes*), and Pallas's and Heuglin's Gulls (*Larus icthyaetus* and *L. heuglini heuglini*). All three species are rare in the south. The causeway also allows close views of the Whimbrel (*Numenius phaeopus*) and Curlew, and at times the Avocet and Crab Plover.

Talaimannar About a kilometre from the now-defunct Talaimannar Customs post there is a 'fishing port'. Large flocks of gulls gather here, including Heuglin's, Brown-headed and Pallas's Gulls.

Sand Banks (Adam's Bridge) A series of islands form what is known as Adam's Bridge, connecting Talaimannar to Rameswaran in the south-west of India. During the breeding season take care not to disturb the hundreds of nesting terns.

Accommodation

Mannar has a few small guest houses and the Palmyrah House – a luxury bungalow.

Opposite: Adam's Peak in the distance seen from Kalametiya.

Below: Garganey, Shoveller and Wigeon take flight in the Vankalai Triangle in Mannar.

Dry Forests

Wilpattu National Park

This national park comprises a complex of lakes called villus, which are surrounded by grassy plains, set within scrub jungle. The biggest draw here is the Leopard. From around 2012 the Leopards in the park began to be comfortable with vehicles, and consequently Wilpattu is now a top site for seeing Leopards. Wilpattu is also good for seeing Sloth Bears.

Wildlife Endemic birds include the Ceylon Junglefowl, Brown-capped Babbler, Ceylon Wood-Shrike and Black-capped Bulbul in riverine habitats. Muntjac or Barking Deer (*Muntiacus muntjak*) are more easily seen in Wilpattu than in any other national park. Butterflies recorded here include the Great Eggfly (*Hypolimnas bolina*), Great Orange-tip, Glad-eye Bushbrown (*Nissanga patnia junonia*), Blue and Common Mormons (*Papilio polytes romulus*), and Common and Crimson Roses. The Sand Lizard is easily seen in sandy areas, especially near the coast.

Getting there The turn-off to Wilpattu National Park is near the 45 km post of the A12. From here, follow the B028 for about 8 km (5 miles).

Accommodation Near the turn-off to Wilpattu off the A12 (Puttalam to Anuradhapura road) is the simple Hotel Leopard Den (formerly the Preshamel Safari Hotel). The nearest for a choice of accommodation is Anuradhapura, which includes the comfortable Palm Garden Village. Day trips are possible from Kalpitiya.

Below: KBFC1, a one-time media Leopard in Yala, in her subadult stage.

Above: *Kudirimalai Point in Wilpattu overlooking the Gulf of Mannar.*

Top right: *Tributaries of the Kala Oya meander through Wilpattu National Park.*

Right: *Spotted Deer run beside one of Wilpattu's famed villus.*

Wasgomuwa National Park

This park is located south of Polonnaruwa and north of the Knuckles Range and Matale foothills. The habitat consists of riverine gallery forest along the Mahaveli and dry monsoon forest in the low foothills.

Wildlife Birds include the Ceylon Junglefowl, Ceylon Grey Hornbill (*Ocyceros gingalensis*), Brown-capped Babbler, Blue-faced Malkoha (*Phaenicophaeus viridirostris*), Lesser Adjutant (*Leptoptilos javanicus*), Grey-headed Fishing Eagle (*Ichthyophaga ichthyaetus*) and Brown Fish-owl. Mammals include the elephant,

Leopard, Sloth Bear, Golden Jackal, Spotted Deer, Sambar (*Cervus Unicolour*), mongooses and civets, as well as the Slender Loris and Hanuman Langur.

Getting there From Kurunegala to Habarana, turn off beyond Galewela onto the Naula Road towards Hettipola. Or from Kandy, from Hasalaka take a minor road north through Handungamuwa.

Accommodation Dunvila Cottage, Willy's Safari Hotel and Wasgomuwa Safari Village are the best-known properties.

Opposite: *A view from Wasgomuwa National Park to the northern slopes of the Knuckles Range.*

Above: *Wasgomuwa has several waterholes, which are great places for seeing mammals, birds and dragonflies.*

Minneriya National Park

The Gathering of elephants (see page 50) peaks here every year between August and September, although the build-up of elephants starts in June and July. This largest concentration of elephants in Asia occurs when the animals gather on the grassland that sprouts on the receding shores of Minneriya Lake. Depending on the levels of water, the safari operators may switch visitors to the nearby Kaudulla National Park, which is similar but is off the Habarana to Trincomalee Road.

Wildlife In the scrub jungle around the lake, endemic birds that may be seen include the Ceylon Junglefowl, Brown-capped Babbler, Ceylon Grey Hornbill and Black-capped Bulbul. The open areas around the lake are good for raptors including the Brahminy Kite (*Haliastur indus indus*), Grey-headed Fish-eagle and majestic White-bellied Sea Eagle (*Haliaeetus leucogaster*). Mammals – apart from elephants, of course – include the endemic Toque Monkey, Hanuman Langur, Grizzled Indian Squirrel, Golden Jackal and Spotted Deer. The Leopard is seen extremely rarely.

Getting There The park entrance is near the 35 km post on the A11 running between Habarana and Polonnaruwa.

Accommodation There are good hotels at Habarana (the nearest), Giritale, Polonnaruwa, Sigiriya and Kandalama.

Opposite: *Minneriya National Park is in the flat lowlands, which have intermittent pockets of hills.*

Right: *A baby elephant squares up to a vehicle.*

Below: *Great Cormorants* (Phalacrocorax carbo) *assume a striking colouration in breeding plumage. They share the lake with Little and Indian Cormorants* (P. fuscicollis).

Yala (Ruhuna) National Park

Yala is undoubtedly Sri Lanka's most visited national park, and the best in Sri Lanka for viewing a wide diversity of animals. It is a wonderful place, with a spectrum of habitats from scrub jungle, lakes and brackish lagoons to riverine areas. Ruhuna National Park is divided into five blocks, of which Block 1 (Yala West) is open to the public. Yala may be closed between 1 September and 15 October.

Left: *Yala's rocky terrain shows evidence of past occupation: note the stupa (a Buddhist shrine containing relics) at the top.*

Opposite: *All of Yala's waterholes in the ground are of human origin. A few natural rock pools also occur.*

Below: *A bull elephant walks past an estuary to an adjoining fresh waterhole.*

Right: Sambar are generally quite wary of people and easily take flight. This stag is preoccupied with succulent waterside plants.

Below: Yala has a few tuskers and they can be reluctant to give way to anyone in their path.

Wildlife The flora is typical of dry monsoon forest vegetation in the southern belt. Plains are interspersed with pockets of forest containing plant species such as the Palu, Satinwood (*Chloroxylon swietenia*), Weera, Maila, Mustard Tree, Neem and Woodapple. Endemic birds include the Ceylon Junglefowl, Brown-capped Babbler, Ceylon Wood-Shrike and Ceylon Swallow. The park is also a good place to see dry-zone specialities like Eurasian and Great Thick-knees, Sirkeer (*Phaenicophaeus leschenaultii leschenaultii*), Blue-faced Malkohas and Malabar Pied Hornbills. It is probably the best place to see the rare Black-necked Stork (*Ephippiorhynchus asiaticus asiaticus*). A day's birding in the park during the northern winter can yield a hundred species.

The biggest draws in Yala are elephants, Leopards and Sloth Bears. A recent study has shown that Yala has one of the highest densities of Leopards in the world. A game drive could yield the Black-naped Hare, Spotted Deer, Sambar, Hanuman Langur, Toque Monkey, Ruddy and Stripe-necked Mongooses (*Herpestes vitticollis*), Wild Pig, Golden Jackal, Land and Water Monitors, and Marsh Crocodile. At the end of the north-east monsoon (February), the park is also a very good place to see butterflies.

Getting there About 40 km (25 miles) beyond Hambantota on the A2.

Accommodation Tissamaharama has a broad range of accommodation. Near the turn-off to the park at Kirinda is the Elephant Reach and a few smaller properties. A successor to the Yala Safari Game Lodge destroyed in the 2004 tsunami is due to re-open. Close to the park is the Chaaya Wild, one of the top game lodges in the country.

Above: A Peafowl takes a dust bath to rid itself of parasites.

Right: Stripe-necked Mongooses are handsomely coloured and the largest of the mongoose species on the island.

Leopard Quest in Yala

27 September

Another incredible day in the park. Driving out of the Yala Village Hotel we paused briefly in front of the lake to have a quick look at the birds. A Spoonbill (*Platalea leucorodia leucorodia*) was present with smaller migrant waders such as Little Stints and Common Greenshanks.

We drove past Palugaswala No. 1 to Palugaswala No. 2. Predictably, the serious photographers were already there. Namal Kamalgoda and Gehan Rajapakse were already in the best position, with five other safari vehicles taking slots behind them. We pulled over parallel to Gehan R. and Namal K., and I extended my tripod head to mount the 600mm f4 lens so that I could shoot over the front of their vehicle. A pack of six Golden Jackals was tearing at a carcass. The animals were nervous. At any given time one would bite a piece of the carcass and rip it out. Some individuals were clambering on top of the carcass, while others just fed from it in a hurried manner.

Some of the jackals looked as though they were young from the last litter to be raised. Once or twice a Spotted Deer alarm call rang out. A more strident call was heard later, followed by a distant Sambar bellowing. A Leopard was clearly on its way. The nervous jackals dispersed. We waited and waited, but no Leopard arrived. A mobile phone call advised us that the Leopard was at Palugaswala No. 1 and the rest of the vehicles sped away. Two vehicles even reversed the 1–2 km (1 mile or so) to No. 1. We decided to wait in case the other subadult of the Kohombagaswala pair came over. The pack of jackals came trotting by again, ran past the carcass and hurried across the road. One paused between us and the carcass and gave me the definitive jackal image.

Opposite, top to bottom: *A Golden Jackal on the prowl breaks into a fast trot; A Great Thick-knee appears to scavenge on flesh, but may in fact be feeding on invertebrates attracted to the rotting carcass.*

Reluctantly we decided to join the pursuit for the Leopard at No. 1 and drove the long loop on the one-way circuit to Palugaswala No. 1.

A Leopard cub had arrived and had apparently been stalking a nearly dead buffalo that was at the waterhole. I suspect that it was hoping to feed off a dead buffalo, but was very wary of one that was still alive. The cub retired to a spot of shade on the embankment and Libby spotted it for us. We decided to wait and take it all in. It was like watching a wildlife film.

A pair of Large-billed or Jungle Crows (*Corvus macrorhynchos culminatus*) began to peck at the carcass. The resident pair of Great Thick-knees was clearly guarding a feeding territory and showed occasional aggression towards the other birds. A Ruddy Mongoose that strayed too close elicited a wing-stretch display. The Ruddy Mongoose backed off. Surprisingly, the one or more Ruddy Mongooses that came did not scavenge on the buffalo. One Great Thick-knee pulled out a piece of meat and I photographed this – it surprised me as up to then I had only seen the birds feeding on insects near the carcass.

A sounder of Wild Pig came in and began to feed on the carcass. There were five of the pigs. The largest was a female, and I suspect they were all females. The Wild Pigs provided some very nice images, albeit of blood and gore.

At least 200 Spotted Deer arrived in groups of around 40 each. The first group was very nervous and initially drank from the muddy edges at the back. The second group drank from the green water that had at least six medium-sized crocodiles in it. Subsequent arrivals seem to know of this and drank from the pool of water closest to the parked jeeps. We watched a crocodile arriving and slithering into the waterhole. The herds of deer included several males – the ones we saw in the last group were very large. Some of the deer were in velvet. I suppose it makes sense for the deer to grow their antlers and build a harem now. The young will arrive after the north-east monsoon rains, which will result in lush grasslands and ample water.

Two deer clashed and one fled. To my amazement, the deer that ran away had full antlers while the victor had none. The deer stood up on their hind legs when fighting. I was just too late to photograph the animals as I had switched off my camera.

Hanuman Langurs were standing sentinel and one barked in alarm. The Spotted Deer also responded. It was clear that a Leopard had arrived but was out of sight. We did later see it.

I was able to photograph the Spotted Deer close to the Hanuman Langurs. I had wanted to take this image for some time to show the association between Hanuman Langurs and Spotted Deer. The two species are often found in the company of each other: the deer benefit from the leaves and fruits dropped by the langurs, while the langurs benefit from the extra pairs of eyes. Over an hour elapsed before the Hanuman Langurs approached the water to drink. By then it was almost 10.30, and we had spent most of the time since 7.30 at the waterhole.

A beautiful male Rose-ringed Parakeet (*Psittacula krameri manillensis*) on a lichen-encrusted dead tree was compositionally outstanding. We had Brahminy Kite, White-bellied Sea Eagle, Grey Heron (*Ardea cinerea*), Painted Stork, Black-winged Stilt and other birds offering close or extended views, which made for some pleasant birdwatching as well. House Swifts (*Apus affinis singalensis*), Crested Tree-Swifts (*Hemiprocne coronata*) and Barn Swallows skimmed the water as they hunted. A Black-headed Ibis foraged about half a metre (1½ ft) away from the crocodiles.

The Leopard moved to another location and we drove out. I had not had a Leopard photography session this morning, but had managed to take a very interesting repertoire of images of animals ranging from Large-billed Crows, Wild Pigs and Golden Jackals feeding on carcasses, to Hanuman Langurs and Spotted Deer lined up to drink water. I had also taken some images of birds and crocodiles. It is amazing what a morning at a waterhole in Yala during the peak of the dry season can yield.

Opposite, clockwise from above left: *A female Orange-breasted Green-pigeon; migrant Blue-tailed Bee-eater; Spotted Deer and Hanuman Langurs.*

Below: *A subadult Leopard exploring its mother's territory.*

Maduru Oya National Park

Maduru Oya has extensive dry-zone forests fringing the Maduru Oya, which was dammed in the 1980s under the accelerated Mahaveli Development project. With the east coast opening to tourism, this park is expected to see more visitors arriving in the future.

Wildlife I spent a lot of time in my youth birdwatching here and was struck by the richness of bird life, which is on a par with other dry-zone national parks such as Wasgamuwa. There are good prospects of seeing elephants. Other mammals to be seen include the Ruddy Mongoose, Spotted Deer and Hanuman Langur. The park is seldom visited and the animals are not habituated to visitors.

Getting there From Polonnaruwa to Arlaganwila, then about 12 km (7½ miles) along the road to Maha Oya, take a right and continue another 8 km (5 miles) to the park entrance. There are also entrances at Heenagala (Mahiyangana-Girandurukotte road) and Galkada (Mahiyangana-Maha Oya road).

Accommodation Polonnaruwa is the nearest (albeit at a distance), with a wide choice. Alternatively, you can take a day trip from the smaller villas and hotels on the east-coast strip from Vakarai to Batticaloa. Small guest houses that are used by locals are located at Mahiyangana, Girandurukotte, Arlaganwila and Maha Oya.

Above: *Grassland and rocky outcrops form part of a patchwork of habitats, making Maduru Oya a rich place for birds and reptiles.*

Opposite: *Maduru Oya was farmed long ago and an ancient dam was unearthed when the location for a new dam was being investigated. Scrub forests have reclaimed the ancient farmland.*

Gal Oya National Park

This park has been in existence for a relatively long time, but is still visited infrequently because of the long access times from the southern half of the island, which was the mainstay of the tourism industry. However, with the development of the east coast for tourism, this park, centred around the great Senanayake Reservoir, will become more visited. Boat rides can be booked from the DWLC office.

Wildlife The tree-studded grasslands around the lakes are good places to see White-bellied Sea Eagles and Grey-headed Fish-eagles. Other raptors found here include the Crested Hawk-Eagle and Serpent Eagle. Lucky visitors have seen elephants swimming across to the islands. Dragonflies include the Lowland Hooktail (*Paragomphus campestris*), which was described as recently as 2013 by Matjaž Bedjanič and is the second of two endemic paragomphids, making it the fourteenth endemic member of 15 species found in Sri Lanka in the family Gomphidae.

Above: A key reason why the Gal Oya National Park was created was to protect the forest that provides a catchment area for the man-made lake, or reservoir, used for irrigation.

Left: Gal Oya is best known for its elephants, which are seen most often when they come to the reservoir for drinking and bathing.

Getting there Entry is from Kossapola, from Inginiyagala. To Inginiyagala take the A31 from Ampara (near the east coast) or turn on to the A4 at Siyambalanduwa (Monaragala-Pottuvil road) and travel via Pallewala and Wadinagala.

Accommodation The old rest house now operates as the Inginiyagala Safari Inn. In Ampara (about 20 km/12½ miles away) is the comfortable Monty Hotel. Between Batticaloa and Pottuvil there are some small hotels and villas (for example Kottukal Beach House), albeit at a distance.

Grassland

Uda Walawe National Park

Uda Walawe is a popular national park because of its elephants and its proximity to Colombo. The park is a mixture of abandoned Teak (*Tectona grandis*) plantations, grassland, scrub jungle and riverine 'gallery forest' along the Walawe Ganga and Mau Ara. Uda Walawe is probably the best place to see wild herds of elephant, consisting of tightly knit family groups of up to four generations of related adult and subadult females and young. It is the only park in the world where you are guaranteed to see a wild elephant on a game drive.

Wildlife Endemic birds include the Ceylon Junglefowl, Ceylon Spurfowl, Ceylon Grey Hornbill, Ceylon Wood-Shrike and Ceylon Swallow. Sirkeer and Blue-faced Malkohas occur in forested areas. The Toque Monkey, Hanuman Langur, Spotted Deer, Wild Pig, Black-naped Hare, Ruddy Mongoose and Sambar are likely to be seen. Leopards are present but rarely seen. Satinwood (*Chloroxylon swietenia*), Ebony (*Diospyros ebenum*) and Trincomalee Wood (*Berrya*

Above: The Uda Walawe reservoir periodically floods.

Left: A pair of Blue-tailed Bee-eaters covers all angles.

cordifolia) trees grow here, and the river margins are characterized by water-loving Kumbuk trees.

Getting there The park entrance is on the B427 between Timbolketiya and Tanamalwila, near the 11 km post. From Colombo take the A8 to Ratnapura, A4 to Pelmadulla and A18 to Timbolketiya.

Accommodation Safari Village at Timbolketiya and Centauria Tourist Hotel at Embilipitiya.

Right: *Ebony trees are found in the dry lowlands.*

Elephants in Uda Walawe

21 July

As soon as the park opened, Ganga Weerasinghe and I travelled in safari vehicles to Thimbirimankada Bungalow, where we met the British High Commissioner Dr Peter Hayes, his wife Kirsty, and his children Libby and Jasper. Birds occuring at Thimbirimankada Wewa included the Large Egret (*Casmerodius albus*), Grey Heron, Black-winged Stilt, Black-headed Ibis and Spoonbill. Raptors seen at the wewa included the Grey-headed Fishing Eagle, White-bellied Sea Eagle, Crested Hawk-Eagle (*Spizaetus cirrhatus ceylanensis*) and Serpent Eagle (*Spilornis cheela spilogaster*). A single Black-winged Kite (*Elanus caeruleus vociferus*) and Oriental Honey-buzzard were seen on the morning and evening game drives respectively. The usual birds seen on the two game drives included the Malabar Pied Hornbill, Jerdon's Bushlark (*Mirafra affinis*), Bar-winged Flycatcher-Shrike (*Hemipus picatus leggei*), Tawny-bellied Babbler, Brown-capped Babbler (heard singing) and Coppersmith Barbet (*Megalaima haemacephala indica*).

At around 3 p.m. a single large bull elephant approached the Thimbirimankada Wewa. Behind it was a family of about ten elephants. The large male came to the water, then crossed over to where we were watching from under a tree. It kept about 60 m (200 ft) away from us. Soon after, the family came to the water and the male joined it, then they left. Another family of about ten elephants came next. As it left another similar-sized family came to the water. After bathing this family dusted itself and left. Soon yet another family arrived. I estimate that at least 40 elephants in four family clans had come and bathed. It was wonderful to watch how they came in, with the adults shielding the young. We also saw about five Wild Pigs.

On the morning game drive we encountered at least three family groups of elephant. We parked close to one that comprised some eleven individuals. Three youngsters slept, lying down. Even the adults were sleeping on their feet, gathered under the shade of a tree. They were at times no more than 7 m (23 ft) away from us and totally relaxed. One looked in poor condition. Later, on the lake bed, we saw 15–20 elephants, some of them alone. Altogether we must have seen 60–80 elephants.

At about 4.15, as we were driving, we witnessed a cobra slithering away near Gonaviddagala. We could also see a single Golden Jackal in the distance, trotting away. Later, when we drove to the lake bed at about 5.20, we saw a group of three Golden Jackals. One had an injured leg and limped away a short distance before sitting down.

We also saw several small herds of Spotted Deer, as well as a single Ruddy Mongoose, and this contributed to a fair sprinkling of mammals on a single day.

Left: *Two bull elephants test each other's strength.*

Opposite, top and bottom: *An elephant herd flanks its young and bunches together for protection;*

Opposite, centre: *Large herds of Water Buffalo compete with other herbivores in the park.*

Montane Forest

Horton Plains National Park

Sri Lanka's second and third highest peaks, Kirigalpotta (2,395 m/7,860 ft) and Thotupola Kanda (2,357 m/7,733 ft), are found here. Three important rivers, the Mahaveli, Kelani and Walawe, originate from Horton Plains. The highlight for walkers is visiting World's End or Baker's Falls.

Wildlife Endemic birds include the Ceylon Whistling Thrush, Ceylon Hill White-eye, Ceylon Wood Pigeon and Dusky-blue Flycatcher. The trees are dominated by Keena, *Syzygium rotundifolium* and *S. sclerophyllum*, and species from the Lauraceae family. Tree Ferns are a conspicuous feature. Butterflies include the Indian Red Admiral, Ceylon Treebrown, and Common and Tamil Treebrowns (*Lethe rohria yoga* and *L. drypetis drypetis*). Numbers of Sambar, the island's largest deer, have soared in the last decade, and there has been a corresponding increase in their main predator, the Leopard. Other mammals include the Wild Pig, Dusky-striped Squirrel and highland races of the Grizzled Indian Squirrel, Toque Monkey and Purple-faced Leaf Monkey.

Getting there From Nuwara Eliya, about 6 km (3¾ miles) from town on the A7, is a left turn towards Ambewala and Pattipola. This continues to the park. From Haputale, take the road via Ohiya.

Accommodation Nuwara Eliya has a wide choice of accommodation.

Knuckles Wilderness

The Knuckles is a remote mountain area which hosts endemic wildlife that is confined to a few mountain peaks in this region. The cardamom cultivation that depleted the natural understorey of the forest is being phased out as part of a conservation programme to preserve the uniqueness of the region. Few people visit this remote area because the roads are bad and accommodation is limited.

Wildlife The vegetation here is tropical submontane forest and is characterized by a Myristica-Cullenia-Aglaia-Litsea community. Endemic birds include the Ceylon Whistling-thrush, Yellow-eared Bulbul, Dusky-blue Flycatcher and Ceylon Hill Myna. The Black Eagle (*Ictinaetus malayensis*) is easily seen and Alpine Swifts (*Tachymarptis melba*) occur in large flocks. Look out for Legge's Hawk Eagle (*Nisaetus kelaarti*). The Leaf-nosed Lizard (*Cerataphora tennentii*), an endemic species restricted to the Knuckles, can be seen easily near Corbett's Gap.

Getting there There are two routes. The highest elevations are reached from Kandy (to the west) or Mahiyangana (to the east) to Loolwatta and then to Corbett's Gap. The easier and better roads are Matale to Rattota to Illukumbura and Riverstone, on a route taken by some to Wasgomuwa National Park. The latter route to the lower elevation northern slopes has gentle slopes compared with the rugged peaks around Corbett's Gap.

Accommodation A few small lodges operate on both routes (for example Kobonillla near Loolwatte). However, most visitors experience the Knuckles Wilderness as a long day trip from a town like Kandy.

Above: *The Knuckles is a complex matrix of rolling plains and rugged mountains creating ecological niches that are occupied by species which are 'point endemics'.*

Opposite: *A scene near Ambewela illustrates how some of the cloud forest has been lost to cattle farming and agricultural use.*

Mammal Watching in Horton Plains

Horton Plains is a good place to see some of the highland races of mammal and to obtain good views of the Sambar, which is difficult to see elsewhere. Since about 2008, Leopards have also shown signs of being less wary of people and have become the top target species for visitors, although the encounter rate for a sighting on daytime visits is probably less than one in 20.

The Sambar is a species that is generally wary of people elsewhere because of hunting pressure. In Uda Walawe National Park there was a time when a pair of Sambar became habituated near a bungalow because it was fed by the bungalow keepers. However, in Yala wild Sambar show little tolerance of visitors, even though other animals like Leopards and elephants have become habituated. By contrast, in Horton Plains the Sambar have become very habituated. The Sambar also epitomizes a good private-public partnership between the Department of Wildlife Conservation and HSBC. Sambar were dying as result of ingesting polythene when they foraged on leftover food. To prevent this, HSBC funded a campaign that has eliminated this threat.

The explosion in numbers of Sambar is due to a combination of factors. One is protection. Another is the escape of a nutrient-rich foreign grass species that was introduced to the cattle farm at Ambewela. The rise in Sambar seems to have resulted in an increase in the population of Leopards. I have heard first-hand accounts of a Leopard stalking Sambar in the middle of the day within sight of picnicking visitors at the Farr Inn Visitor Centre. In the evening I have on a few occasions heard attempts by Leopard to hunt Sambar, and seen Sambar bunching up and sending stags to ward off the threat.

The highland race of the Toque Macaque has long toque hairs on the head.

A Sambar showing the scent gland beneath its eyes.

Night-time is also the best time to see the widespread Black-naped Hare, of which Sri Lanka has an endemic subspecies. It is probably not rare, but I have never seen one during the day. Other observers on night excursions have also recorded the Ring-tailed Civet. The Wild Pig is a further species that is nocturnal. This is almost certainly due to it still being hunted by people for food. It is probably not as rare as one may think, and its presence is often evident in it having rooted about in the soil in search of food.

The Muntjac or Barking Deer occurs in the park (my sightings of it have been in the early mornings or evenings at the Ambewela Cattle Farm). The deer can be made out on the short-cropped grass that they have entered from the adjoining cloud forest. As the sun comes up they melt into the cloud forest.

Not quite a deer, but superficially similar and in it is own family, is the mouse-deer. Sri Lanka has two species in the lowlands, the White-spotted (*Moschiola meminna*) and the endemic Yellow-striped Mouse-deer. The Mountain Mouse-deer is possibly an endemic and is pending description. In 2010 I photographed an encounter between a Brown

The Brown Mongoose is a successful carnivore that ranges from Colombo to the highest cloud forests.

Mongoose and a Mountain Mouse-deer (*Moschiola* sp.). Another mongoose found in the park is the Badger or Stripe-necked Mongoose. It has beautiful markings and is the largest of the four mongoose species on the island. I would say that for casual visitors the strike rate for seeing Brown and Stripe-necked Mongooses is loosely in the order of 1/20 and 1/10 respectively.

The Purple-faced Leaf Monkey occurs in four forms, and the highland form, known as the Bear Monkey, has a shaggy coat. The monkeys remain shy in the park, but habituated troops can be encountered at the Hakgala Botanical Gardens. Toque Monkeys have been recorded by visitors to Horton Plains National Park. The highland race (*Macaca sinica opisthomelas*) has long hair that extends over the eyes on its toque or cap. Toque Monkeys are numerous at certain archaeological sites in the dry lowlands, and it is easy to believe that they are common. However, in primary forests even in the lowlands, they are not so numerous and tend to frequent areas close to rivers. They could be naturally scarce in Horton Plains, where less food is available. They are, however, easy to see at the Hakgala Botanical Gardens, where habituated troops are fed by visitors.

The star primate here is the Horton Plains Slender Loris, which is awaiting description as a new species. It had not been seen for several decades until primatologist Dr Anna Nekaris spotlighted it in 2002. In 2010 it was photographed for the first time at a site close to Nuwara Eliya by a research team funded by the Zoological Society of London.

Three species of squirrel can be seen in the park. The diminutive Ceylon Dusky-striped Squirrel was until recently treated as a subspecies of the form found on the Indian mainland. In 2011 it was split into an endemic species. This seems to be the most abundant of the squirrels in the park. The highland form of the Giant or Grizzled Indian Squirrel is also found here. It has black upperparts and yellow underparts. The highland form has white frosting on the tail. The other squirrel is the Flame-striped or Layard's Squirrel, which is another recent split. There is a reasonable likelihood of seeing at least one of these species if a day is spent in the park, quietly observing its wildlife. The highland race of the Palm Squirrel may be seen in the more disturbed areas of the park. This means that all four species of Sri Lankan squirrel may be observed in the park. The split of the two squirrels, together with other recent splits, raised the number of endemic mammal species in Sri Lanka to 21.

A few visitors have been treated to a Eurasian Otter (*Lutra lutra*) swimming nonchalantly at Arrenga Pool. It is generally a shy animal, and it is possible that the majority of the otter sightings at Arrenga Pool may relate to a single confident individual.

Mammal watching in Horton Plains is harder than in the national parks in the dry lowlands, but it has its own rewards – endemic mammals in beautiful cloud forest and rolling plains that fall off at the edge of the Earth.

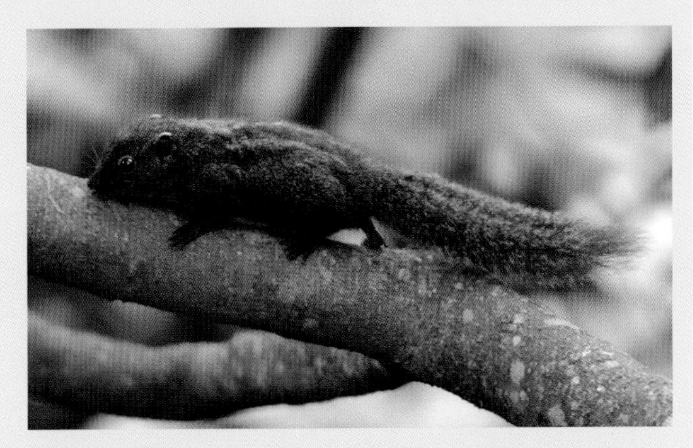

The Ceylon Dusky-striped Squirrel can be furtive.

Bodhinagala

Bodhinagala is a relatively small tract of secondary lowland rainforest, with a Buddhist hermitage located centrally. It is surprisingly rich floristically and holds a number of endemic fauna within relatively easy reach of the commercial capital of Colombo.

Wildlife Bodhinagala's claim to fame with birders is as a reliable site for the endemic Green-billed Coucal. It also contains a number of other endemics such as the Ceylon Spurfowl, Yellow-fronted Barbet, Ceylon Small Barbet (*Megalaima rubricapilla*), Black-capped Bulbul and Spot-winged Thrush, and subcontinental endemics such as the Ceylon Frogmouth (*Batrachostomus moniliger*) and Malabar Trogon. Butterflies include the Tawny Rajah. The endemic Purple-faced Leaf and Toque Monkeys, and Grizzled Indian Squirrel are the more visible of the mammals.

Getting there The turn-off to Bodhinagala is just before the 29 km post on the A8 (Ratnapura Road).

Accommodation Using private transport, the site can be visited as a half-day trip from Colombo, which has a wide choice of accommodation.

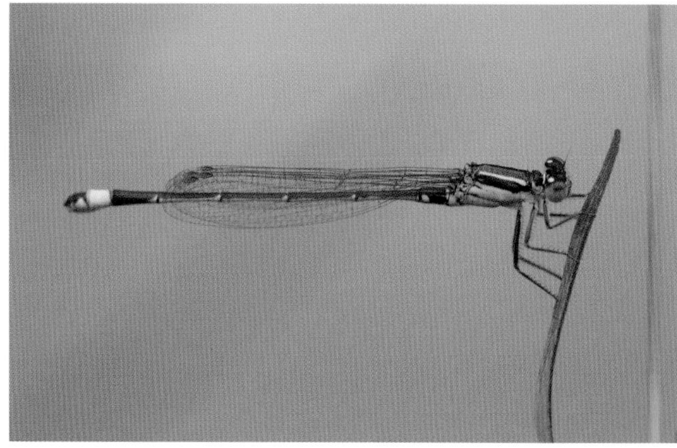

Top: *The Ceylon Hill White-eye showing the 'split' eye-ring.*

Above: *The Mountain Reedling is a 'spreadwing' which does not do so.*

Left: *Bodhinagala is an important rainforest due to its high biodiversity as well as its relative proximity to the capital and its well-maintained road, which makes it easy to experience the rainforest.*

Above: *The Oriental Dwarf Kingfisher is seen regularly at Bodhinagala.*

Left: *A* Cnemaspis *sp. gecko, one of several diurnal geckos.*

Below left: *A tangle of lianas.*

Below: *An endemic Tiger Beetle (*Calochroa discrepans*) which has been recorded in the wet and dry zones.*

Sinharaja Rainforest

The Sinharaja Man and Biosphere Reserve was declared a World Heritage Site in 1988. It is arguably the most important biodiversity site in Sri Lanka and is also internationally important for tropical biodiversity. It is famous for its bird waves (see pages 60 and 184). Sinharaja comprises lowland and submontane wet evergreen forests with submontane Patana grasslands in the east. A staggering 64 per cent of the tree species are endemic to Sri Lanka. The lower slopes and valleys have remnant dipterocarpus forest, with the middle and higher slopes characterized by trees of the genus *Mesua*. Orchids (*Orchidaceae* spp.) and pitcher plants (*Nepenthaceae* spp.) are common in nutrient-poor soils.

Top right: *The Serendib Scops-owl favours secondary growth.*

Centre right: *Juvenile Ceylon Junglefowl use cryptic camouflage.*

Bottom right: *The female Malabar Trogon lacks the male's red breast.*

Below: *A Ceylon Hanging-parrot feeding on the nectar of a* Loranthus *sp.*

Wildlife Endemic birds include the Ceylon Spurfowl, Ceylon Junglefowl, Ceylon Wood Pigeon, Ceylon Hanging-parrot, Layard's Parakeet, Red-faced Malkoha, Green-billed Coucal, Serendib Scops-owl, Chestnut-backed Owlet, Ceylon Grey Hornbill, Yellow-fronted Barbet, Ceylon Small Barbet, Greater Flameback (*Chrysocolaptes stricklandi*), Black-capped Bulbul, Spot-winged Thrush, Ceylon Rufous and Brown-capped Babblers, Ashy-headed Laughingthrush, Ceylon Blue Magpie, White-faced Starling, Ceylon Hill Myna (*Gracula ptilogenys*), Ceylon Scaly Thrush, Ceylon Scimitar Babbler (*Pomatorhinus [schisticeps] melanurus*) and Ceylon Crested Drongo. Indian subcontinental endemics include the Malabar Trogon and Ceylon Frogmouth.

Half of Sri Lanka's endemic mammals and butterflies are found here. Visitors may see the Purple-faced Leaf Monkey and Grizzled Indian Squirrel. Endemic lizards include the Whistling Lizard (*Calotes liolepis*) as well as the Rough-nosed Horned Lizard (*Ceratophora aspera*).

Getting there Access is possible from Pitadeniya, but not practical for most visitors. Motorable access is to Kudawa via Ratnapura or via Buluthota Pass from Yala or via Katukurunda Junction, Agalawatta and Kalawana from the coast.

Accommodation Boulder Garden at Kalawana and Rainforest Edge at Veddagala provide the nearest star-quality accommodation. Serious birders can look at Martin's and Blue Magpie Lodge, near the reserve.

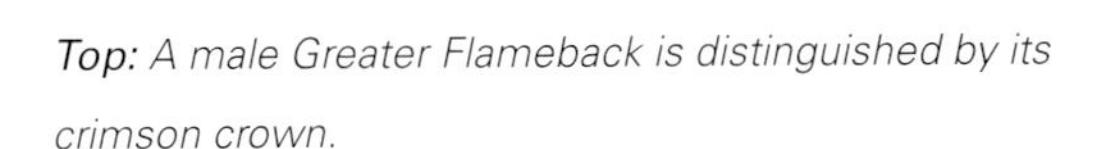

Top: A male Greater Flameback is distinguished by its crimson crown.

Right: The Whistling Lizard is a shy endemic.

Animal Encounters in Sinharaja

5 July

Foraging on the ground near the bird table of the newly built visitor centre was a habituated Emerald Dove (*Chalcophaps indica robinsoni*), as well as a pair of Spot-winged Thrushes. On the way up to the barrier gate, we came across a small bird wave that consisted of three Crested Drongos and a few Ceylon Rufous Babblers. A few Scarlet Minivets (*Pericrocotus flammeus flammeus*) and Black-naped Monarchs were loosely associated. A pair of Ceylon Scimitar Babblers was present and gave good views. We checked into Martin's Simple Lodge late in the afternoon. It was bright and sunny throughout most of the day, except for a short burst of rain for a few minutes at around 4.55 p.m.

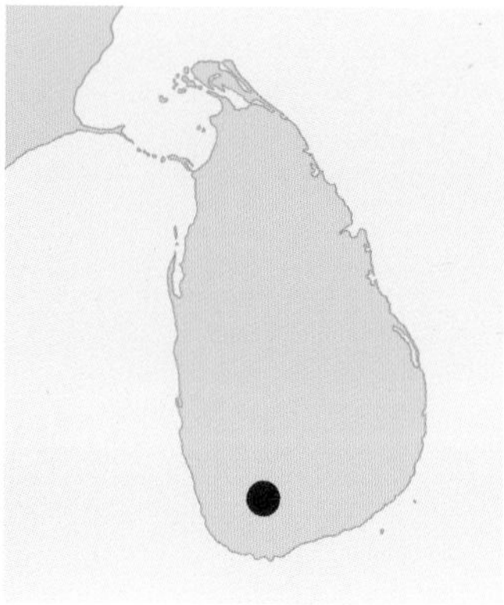

We encountered another bird wave just after the barrier gate at about 4 p.m. Four Brown-capped Babblers foraged on the ground, offering clear views. A single Red-faced Malkoha flew and perched high over us, providing a good view. Also present were Ceylon Crested Drongos, Ceylon Rufous Babblers, Ashy-headed Laughingthrush and Layard's Parakeets, which flew away. A single Layard's Squirrel followed the flock. The first flock we saw also included a Layard's Squirrel.

After a burst of rain we came to the waterhole (Maguruwala). We had just missed a bird wave that had crossed, only seeing a Greater Flameback, the last to cross.

Just beyond the waterhole we followed a pair of Malabar Trogons that flew beside the track. Only the Striped Rasbora (*Rasbora daniconius*) was visible in the poor light at the waterhole. The Sri Lanka Water Snakes (*Xenochrophis asperrimus*) could not be seen.

On our return journey at about 5.30 we came across four Ceylon Wood Pigeons between the barrier gate and the first pond. Two were chasing each other. They offered extended views as they flew around and foraged on fruit. This is the place where wood pigeons are usually seen. We heard the call of a Brown Wood Owl (*Strix leptogrammica indranee*), and later on the call of a Chestnut-backed Owlet. As we approached the barrier, we encountered another small bird wave and two scimitar babblers that showed themselves well. We had comes across four bird waves on this day.

The Black-capped Bulbul, Crested Drongo, Ceylon Scimitar Babbler, Ceylon Rufous Babbler, Brown-capped Babbler, Ashy-headed Laughingthrush, Layard's Parakeet, Ceylon Hill Myna, Legge's Flowerpecker, Spot-winged Thrush, Red-faced Malkoha and Greater Flameback were among the endemic birds seen today. With the Chestnut-backed Owlet that we heard, the total number of endemic birds encountered was 13.

We also saw more than a dozen Kangaroo Lizards, ranging from very small juveniles to several displaying adults whose heads had turned a glossy green and rear legs showed orange on the dorsal surface. One displayed, with its gular sac and nuchal crest erected. The highlight was a Hump-nosed Lizard spotted by our guide near the wood-pigeon location. This is where I had seen this species previously – it is surprising that this is only my second record here in so many years. The light was very low and most of my photographs were soft. The lizard opened its mouth slightly and I could just make out the red lining inside its mouth. It opens its mouth fully when it needs to intimidate intruders with a sign of aggression. I approached it slowly to photograph it, then carefully moved away. After I left, it ran down and clambered up another tree further away and displayed. We did not see any Green Garden Lizards.

***Opposite, clockwise from top left:** Brown-capped Babbler; Red-faced Malkoha; Ceylon Scimitar Babbler; Striped Rasbora; Black-capped Bulbul; Kangaroo Lizard.*

The pond at the visitor centre is nicely done. Perched around it were Indigo and Crimson Dropwings, and Spine-tufted Skimmers. At one of the streams before the barrier gate, I photographed a pair of mating Marsh Skimmers (*Orthetrum luzonicum*). I was photographing the male when the guide pointed out the female close to it. The pair engaged in tandem and stayed together for more than five minutes. They moved position occasionally if, for example, an ant disturbed them. The species can be distinguished from the similar Asian Skimmer by its clear wing bases. Black-tipped Flashwings were also present at the stream.

An obliging Plum Judy (*Abisara echerius prunosa*) allowed close photography, although it moved around. Clipper and Commander (*Moduza procris calidasa*) and Grass Yellow sp, Tree Nymph and several Blue Mormons were seen. At about 7.15, when we were driving back to Colombo, we saw a Blue Mormon that appeared to be asleep. It was on top of a leaf and had its wings fully open.

A few Giant Wood Spider webs were seen, one with about five males on it. The False Lanternflies (*Pyrops maculata*) were on the same Mora tree that they are usually seen on. They are confined to forests and uncommon.

Besides the Layard's Squirrels that were following the bird flocks, the only other mammal seen today was a small, shy troop of Purple-faced Leaf Monkeys, of the western race that is found here.

Above: *The unmarked wing bases of the Marsh Skimmer distinguish it from the similar Asian Skimmer.*

Below: *A female Giant Wood Spider, common in Sinharaja.*

Kithulgala (Kelani Valley) Rainforest

Kithulgala (Kelani Valley Forest Reserve) was established to protect the watershed of the Kelani River. It is home to much of Sri Lanka's endemic fauna and flora. Kithulgala is also known as the location for the filming of the classic film *The Bridge on the River Kwai*.

Wildlife A good number of endemic birds, including the Spot-winged Thrush, Green-billed Coucal, Red-faced Malkoha, Ceylon Grey Hornbill, Yellow-fronted Barbet, Ceylon Spurfowl, Ceylon Rufous Babbler, Ceylon Scimitar Babbler and Ceylon Frogmouth, are found here. Mammals include the Grizzled Indian Squirrel and Layard's Striped Squirrel. The streams hold endemic fish and amphibians, and the Kangaroo Lizard is frequently seen.

Getting there The Kithulgala Rest House is just after the 37 km post on the A7. Take the ferry across the river and access the forest using the village trails.

Accommodation The Kithulgala Rest House and Plantation Hotel have hot-water showers. Rafter's Retreat and Sisira's River Lounge are more basic.

Above: Grey Hornbills are important dispersers of seeds.

Left: Birders take the ferry at Kithulgala.

The Rainforests of Galle

Many people, including Sri Lankans, are not aware of Galle's potential to be a gateway to Sri Lanka's lowland rainforests. Its image in a tourism context is usually that of a Dutch fortress city; a piece of living history.

Naturalists have known for a long time that small but valuable remnants of rainforest such as the Kottawa Arboretum and Hiyare Rainforest Park are just over half an hour away from Galle. Kanneliya, one of the largest tracts of lowland rainforest, is only an hour and 15 minutes away. What has made rainforest tourism a strong possibility are the laudable attempts of the Forest Department and the Galle Municipality to encourage ecotourism, especially their efforts to create ease of access for visitors in terms of entering the forests by ticketed entry. Access in terms of road infrastructure has always been available to a certain degree.

Travelling to Galle along the coastline affords vistas of waves tossing and turning on golden beaches. Fishing communities can still be seen gathering in crowds to haul in the catch when the fishing fleet returns after a night out at sea. Galle is a living heritage city, heralding five centuries of turbulent conflict with Europeans ever since a Portuguese armada sailed in by accident. Ethnographically, Galle's southerners have their own character, with slight nuances in their customs and manners.

There is, however, more to Galle than the people, the golden coastline and the colonial history. It is also a gateway to some of the largest remaining tracts of lowland rainforest, considered to be the richest in south Asia. Of these, the most important is the Kanneliya-Nakiyadeniya-Dediyagala forest reserve complex, simply referred to as Kanneliya. Galle can also be used as a gateway through Deniyaya to enter the famous Sinharaja through its southern boundaries. Only time will tell whether plans to develop Galle as

Above: Yellow-browed Bulbuls are common in forests.

Top: Ceylon Hanging-parrots frequent treetops, so eye-level views are only possible if the tree is growing on a slope below.

Opposite: Secondary rainforest has a dense undergrowth.

a major port and a point of decentralization for the south will materialize, but there is absolutely no doubt that the last remaining large rainforests should be preserved for all time.

The area from Hikkaduwa to Galle has a wide range of accommodation, from rooms let to backpackers to some of the most upmarket hotels in the country. Galle has become the southern Riviera of Sri Lanka, with the Galle Fort having some of the most chic and exclusive villas and boutique hotels in the country. Galle Fort and Unawatuna both have some excellent cafes where you can go for a nice meal after whale watching or a trip to the rainforest.

Kottawa Rainforest and Arboretum

The Kottawa Arboretum is a small tract of lowland secondary rainforest that holds a surprising number of endemic species. It is a part of the Kottawa-Kombala Conservation Forest of 1,800 ha (4,500 acres).

Wildlife For a small place, this is very good for endemic birds, including the Spot-winged Thrush, Ceylon Spurfowl, Ceylon Hanging-parrot, Layard's Parakeet, Ceylon Small Barbet, Legge's Flowerpecker, Black-capped Bulbul, Ceylon Grey Hornbill, Chestnut-backed Owlet, Yellow-fronted Barbet and even the potential split, the Ceylon Hill Munia (*Lonchura kelaarti*). Hard to see but found here is the subcontinental endemic Sri Lanka Frogmouth. Bag loads of forest birds are found here to tempt you to leave a sunny beach in Galle, including the Yellow-browed Bulbul (*Iole indica indica*), Asian Paradise Flycatcher, Emerald Dove, Green Imperial Pigeon, Scarlet Minivet, Ceylon Scimitar Babbler and Dark-fronted Babbler. Look out for the Ceylon Crested or Greater Racket-tailed Drongo, which should give itself away by its usual garrulous habits. This is in the frame to be split one day as a good species, which would make it another endemic to Sri Lanka.

The endemic Purple-faced Leaf Monkey and Grizzled Indian Squirrel are the mammals you are

Right: A young Toque Macaque uses its throat pouches to hoard food in case it has to take flight.

Far right: The Hiyare Reservoir and Reserve are close to the town of Galle.

most likely to see. Mammals like the Sambar and Muntjac are also present, but quite shy. Endemic reptiles found here include the Kangaroo Lizard, which is relatively easy to see. Kottawa is also a good place for the spectacular Hump-nosed Lizard. A displaying male with his extended gular sac is a dramatic sight. Much harder to see in the leaf litter is the Rough-nosed Horned Lizard.

The Kottawa Rainforest and Arboretum is very rich in floristic diversity. The vegetation comprises impressive stands of endemic Hora (*Dipterocarpus* spp.) trees, which rise up to 45 m (148 ft) in height. You may also see the endemic Pelan (*Putranjiva zeylanica*), Kataboda, Malaboda and Welipiyanna (*Anisophyllea cinnamomoides*). Among the trees that carry name boards, look out for the Diya Na (*Mesua ferrea*), Dorana (*Dipterocarpus glandulosus*), Kataboda, Malaboda (*Myristica ceylanica*) and Pelan. Some of the flora that you might see in the understorey includes the Gal Karandha (*Humbodltia laurifolia*), Beru (*Agrostistachys coriacea*) and Tapassara Bulath (*Apama* sp.). Look out for the Dorana that is labelled on the trail. The sap from the bark is used as a varnish for statues, especially for those of the Lord Buddha.

Getting there From Galle take the Udugama Road, the B129, opposite the turn to the Closenberg Hotel and the Galle Port (which you pass on the right if you were heading to Matara). Just past the 13 km post on the B129, on the right, is the Kottawa Information Centre. Buy your entrance tickets here. Further along the road before the 14 km post are gates to the left and a large yellow sign 'Kottawa Arboretum Wet Evergreen Forest Kottawa Kombala'. Enter the forest here and follow the wide trail that runs parallel to the road until it rejoins it about 1 or 2 km (about 1 mile) further down. From Galle town it is about 16 km (10 miles) to the ticket office; approximately half an hour's drive.

Hiyare Rainforest Park

Hiyare (more formally the Environment and Biodiversity Study Centre and Botanical Garden) is

a reservoir bordered by 245 ha (600 acres) of secondary lowland rainforest. The reservoir was established in 1911 and encompasses 22 ha (55 acres). It is managed by staff of the Galle Municipality. The Forest Department also has jurisdiction, as the reservoir adjoins the Kottawa-Kombala Forest Reserve. This should not be confused with the Kottawa Rainforest and Arboretum, which is a few kilometres further down along the Udugama Road (B129). Volunteers from the Wildlife Conservation Society in Galle are at the site on most weekdays, and almost always at weekends. They are often happy to assist visitors, and have a small museum and library at the site.

Wildlife A realistic idea of what birds can be seen can be gauged from a visit in the month of September by Hasantha Lokugamage and myself. Birds heard (h) or seen included the Ceylon Spurfowl (h), Brown-capped Babbler (h), Spot-winged Thrush (h), Black-capped Bulbul, Ceylon Grey Hornbill, Ceylon Hanging-parrot, Spotted Dove (*Streptopelia chinensis ceylonensis*), Green Imperial Pigeon, Orange-breasted Green Pigeon (*Treron bicincta leggei*), Black-headed Cuckoo-Shrike (h) (*Coracina melanoptera sykesi*), Red-vented Bulbul, Yellow-browed Bulbul, Purple-rumped Sunbird, Pale-billed Flowerpecker (*Dicaeum erythrorhynchos ceylonense*), Black-naped Monarch, Tickell's Blue Flycatcher (*Cyornis tickelliae jerdoni*), Scarlet Minivet, Alexandrine Parakeet (*Psittacula eupatria eupatria*), Rose-ringed Parakeet, Dark-fronted Babbler, White-bellied Drongo, Greater Flameback, Black-rumped Flameback (h), Brown-headed Barbet, Common Iora, Red-wattled Lapwing (*Vanellus indicus lankae*), Little Cormorant and Indian Pond Heron (*Ardeola grayii grayii*).

Mammals likely to be seen by visitors include the Indian Grizzled or Giant Squirrel. This is the black and yellow, wet-zone race *melanochra*. Sightings of the Palm Squirrel, Toque Monkey and Purple-faced Leaf Monkey are also possible. Other mammals recorded in the reserve include the Golden Palm Civet (*Paradoxurus hermaphroditus*) and Sambar. Butterflies include the Blue Mormon, Common Sailor, Crimson Rose, Bluebottle and Blue Oakleaf.

Hiyare is a part of the southern Sinharaja-Hiniduma-Kanneliya plant community. The dominant tree of the rainforest is the Hora, a member of the Dipterocarpaceae family. The Malaboda and Kekiriwara are two other common rainforest species. The Weval, a *Calamus* vine, is present. These vines are much depleted in Sri Lankan rainforests due to unsustainable harvesting. The Venivel or Tree Turmeric (*Coscinium fenestratum*) is a locally well-known medicinal creeper and is widespread in the forest. The trunks of tall trees are often clothed with *Freycinetia walkeri*.

Getting there From Galle take the Udugama Road (B129). See Kottawa Arboretum (opposite) for more details. A hundred metres past the 9 km post of the B129, take the road to the right; 4.4 km (2¾ miles) later you come to a big bridge. Take the dirt track immediately to your left; this leads to the Hiyare Reservoir 100 m (300 ft) away. From Galle town, it is 17 km (10½ miles). Allow half an hour for the journey.

Kanneliya Forest Reserve

Formally known as the Kanneliya-Dediyagala-Nakiyadeniya Forest Complex (KDN Complex), this is an excellent forest reserve of logged secondary forest with virgin forest in the interior and forest ridges. From the entrance gate there is a wide-access track and open forest allowing good views into the interior. Kanneliya's importance as a biodiversity reservoir is on par with Sinharaja's. It is a jewel in Sri Lanka's biodiversity crown.

The fauna is similar to that in Sinharaja, but the flora has its own distinctive characteristics. The reserve is made up of the three contiguous reserves of Kanneliya, Dediyagala and Nakiyadeniya, but is often simply referred to as Kanneliya. The large area has made it possible for viable populations of the larger mammals, including top-level predators like the Leopard, to remain.

The reserve straddles the Galle and Matara Districts and comprises a total of 10,139 ha/25,053 acres (Kanneliya 5,306 ha/13,111 acres, Dediyagala 3,504 ha/8,658 acres and Nakiyadeniya 1,329 ha/3284 acres). The altitude varies from 60 to 425 m (200 to 1,400 ft). The average temperature is 27 °C (80.6 °F). The wettest months are historically May to June and October to November, but bear in mind that rainfall patterns have changed dramatically in the past few years. The underlying geology comprises khondalites and charnockites. The forest is an important catchment for the Gin Ganga (River) and Nilwala Ganga (River).

Wildlife Open forest makes this a good site to look for the Ceylon Spurfowl. Other birds recorded here include the Ceylon Hanging-parrot, Green-billed Coucal, Red-faced Malkoha, Ceylon Blue Magpie, Brown-capped Babbler, Yellow-fronted Barbet, Ceylon Small Barbet, Spot-winged Thrush, Legge's Flowerpecker, Black-capped Bulbul, Ceylon Hill Myna, Ceylon Crested Drongo, Brown Fish-owl, Indian Blue Robin, Brown-capped Pygmy Woodpecker (*Dendrocopus nanus gymnopthalmos*), Oriental or

Black-backed Dwarf Kingfisher (*Ceyx erithacus erithacus*), Stork-billed Kingfisher (*Halcyon capensis capensis*), Scarlet Minivet and Crested Serpent Eagle.

Kanneliya contains a good selection of mammals, including the Leopard, Sambar, Muntjac, Crested Porcupine, Wild Pig, Tranvancore or Small Flying Squirrel (*Petinomys fuscocapillus*), Slender Loris and occasionally Asian Elephant. The mammals most likely to be seen by visitors are the endemic Purple-faced Leaf Monkey and Toque Monkey, and the Grizzled Indian Squirrel. The wet-zone race of this squirrel is black and yellow; despite the strong colouration it is well camouflaged in the shady canopy.

Endemic lizards to be seen here include the Rough-nosed Horned Lizard and Hump-nosed Lizard. Some beautiful and harmless Sri Lankan snakes can also be seen here, including the Green Whip Snake, Gunther's Bronzeback (*Dendrelaphis caudolineolatus*) and Common Bronzeback. The Python and endemic Green Pit Viper are also present, but are often difficult to see. The streams in Kanneliya harbour a variety of endemic freshwater fish such as the Cherry Barb, Black Ruby Barb (*Puntius nigrofasciatus*), Stone Sucker, Paradise Combtail and many more. Butterflies include the Commander, Rustic (*Cupha erymanthis placida*), Clipper, Common Bluebottle and the tigers. Dragonflies include the Black-tipped Flashwing, which is common along fast-flowing streams, and the Sri Lanka Iris Cascader.

Getting there Proceed as to the Kottawa Arboretum (see page 190) on the Udugama Road (B129). Continue along the B129 to a T-junction at Udugama, locally referred to as the Bar Handiya (*handiya* means junction), just past the 32 km post. Take the right-turn sign posted to Hiniduma and get onto the B429. The turn-off to Kanneliya is about 300 m (984 ft) after the 3 km post on the B429. The last 1.4 km (3/4 mile) are along a small, winding dirt track. Vehicles such as tourist vans and coaches have to be left on the B429, but bear in mind that road access may be improved in future. From Galle town to Kanneliya it is 44 km (27 miles). Allow 1½ hours from Galle for the drive.

An interesting plant is the Gal Karandha. Its leaves look quite normal on a casual inspection, but if the plant nodes are split they are found to be hollow and contain ant colonies. The ants and the trees have a symbiotic relationship.

The National Conservation Review (NCR) conducted between 1991 and 1996 surveyed 204 forests, including the KDN complex. The NCR recorded 319 woody plants, of which 159 are endemic species. Conspicuous trees in Kanneliya include the Kataboda (*Cullenia rosayroana*), Kekuna (*Canarium zeylanicum*), Welipiyanna (*Anisophyllea cinnamomoides*), Dombakeena (*Calophyllum moonii*), Godapara (*Dillenia retusa*), Beraliya, Thiniya (*Shorea* sp.), Ariddha (*CampnoSperma zeylanicum*) and Etamba (*Mangifera zeylanica*). Thambatu Val and Ma Weval are two *Calamus* vines that are traditionally harvested for making baskets and furniture

Above: *A close view of Forsten's Cat Snake (*Boiga forsteni*) will show the cat-like vertical pupils.*

Above left: *The Green Vine Snake is a harmless and elegant tree-climbing species.*

Opposite: *The Gal Karandha, an endemic to the Western Ghats and Sri Lanka, is easily seen in Kanneliya. It is one of many plants that have an association with ants.*

Information for Visitors

When to Travel

Sri Lanka has pronounced climatic zones with their own seasonal variations, so despite being a fairly small country the climate does not lend itself to sweeping generalizations. Because of the climatic variations there is usually some part of the country that is dry and enjoying good weather. The period from January to April marks the warm, dry season in the western lowlands. As the endemic wildlife-rich wet zone in the west is also at its driest, this is the preferred time for birders. In the highlands at Nuwara Eliya, and especially Horton Plains, it can be dry but cold. There may be frost in the highlands in January and February. The best time for visiting birdwatchers is from November to April, with February being a good month because it is largely dry. During this period migrants are present, adding to the tally of birds.

Wildlife viewing in the national parks in the dry zone is best between May and September, when it is dry and hot and animals are concentrated around waterholes, with streams reduced to a mere trickle. The downside is that the parks can be very dusty. The north-east monsoon from October to January makes parks such as Minneriya and Kaudulla inaccessible, but other parks such as Yala, despite receiving rain, remain accessible. The monsoons also influence the whale-watching and diving seasons. Mirissa in the south and Kalpitiya in the west are best from around December to mid-April, and Trincomalee on the east is best from March to September. See also the wildlife-watching calendar (page 20), which indicates the best months for the top target species.

Organized Wildlife Travel

It is not recommended that you drive yourself in Sri Lanka. Bear in mind that the travel time between locations cannot be gauged from a map. Joining an organized tour or having a tour tailored for you can save a lot of time and trouble. In Sri Lanka qualified tourist guides who speak good English are available. Having one who is also a naturalist will make a huge difference to what you see. Some hotels also have resident naturalists who can be booked for excursions. The official guides provided in the national parks and reserves are often not good naturalists. The better ones and some of the safari-vehicle drivers know their birds.

Organized tours A number of companies around the world operate package tours to Sri Lanka. These may not always be convenient for families with young children or for those for whom mammals and other natural history may be a priority. For those with specific needs it is best to book with a tour operator who can tailor a tour. A number of tour companies in Sri Lanka can organize a package incorporating mammals and other natural history, culture and even chilling out on a beach, all tailored to individual requests. Although this should not be treated as an endorsement, I have listed a few below which have good reputations. Some are long-standing companies that also offer wildlife tours, while others are relatively new companies with a strong focus on natural history. Some are specialist subsidiaries of the big names in the travel industry, and others are single-owner/manager companies. Almost all are based in Colombo. Broadly speaking, if you book a tour with a company licensed by the Sri Lanka Tourism Development Authority and one that uses licensed, experienced guides, progress will be smooth. Some tour operators are also members of the Sri Lanka Inbound Tour Operators Association.

A Baur & Co. (Travels), www.baurs.com
Aitken Spence Travels, www.aitkenspencetravels.com
Bird and Wildlife Team,
 www.birdandwildlifeteam.com
Birdwing Nature Holidays, www.birdwingnature.com
Eco Team (Mahoora Tented Safaris),
 www.srilankaecotourism.com
Hemtours (Diethelm Travel Sri Lanka),
 www.hemtours.com
High Elms Travel, www.highelmstravel.com

Jetwing Eco Holidays, www.jetwingeco.com
Lanka Sportreizen, www.lsr-srilanka.com
Little Adventures, www.littleadventuressrilanka.com
Nature Trails, www.naturetrails.lk
Quickshaws Tours, www.quickshaws.com
Red Dot, www.reddottours.com
Sri Lanka in Style, www.srilankainstyle.com
Walkers Tours, www.walkerstours.com
Walk with Jith, www.walkwithjith.com

International travel companies There are many international travel companies that will tailor specialist wildlife tours, quite often with one of the companies listed above as the ground agent. I have listed just a few of the better known ones that have a special angle in connection with Sri Lanka.

Nature Trek, www.naturetrek.com
The Whale and Dolphin Company,
www.whale-and-dolphin.com
Wildlife Worldwide, www.wildlifeworldwide.com

Sample Itineraries

Big-game Safari (9 nights/10 days)

The main objective of this itinerary is to see Sri Lanka's big five: the Blue Whale, Sperm Whale, Asian Elephant, Leopard and Sloth Bear.

Day 1 Arrive in Sri Lanka and transfer to Colombo for one night. Afternoon, walk in Talangama Wetland for Black and Yellow Bitterns, Watercock and common birds and dragonflies.

Day 2 After breakfast, leave to Uda Walawe for one night. Afternoon game drive to Uda Walawe, where sightings of Asian Elephant are guaranteed.

Day 3 After breakfast, leave to Yala National Park for three nights. Afternoon game drive to Yala in search of Yala's big three – the Leopard, Sloth Bear and Asian Elephant. Yala has one of the highest densities of Leopards in the world. Due to the lack of other large carnivores the Leopard is the top predator and adults and cubs are remarkably relaxed during the day, offering great opportunities for viewing and photography. Yala is also the best place in Asia for sighting the shy and usually nocturnal Sloth Bear, and is also home to more than 250 Asian Elephants, with the highlight being the 10–12 large tuskers that roam around the park. The park is also good for dry-zone birds like Eurasian and Great Thick-knees, Sirkeer and Blue-faced Malkohas, and Malabar Pied Hornbill. A day's birding in the park during the northern winter can yield 100 species.

Days 4–5 Morning and afternoon safaris in Yala in search of the Leopard, Sloth Bear and Asian Elephant.

Day 6 Morning, one last game drive in Yala. After breakfast, leave to Galle for three nights. Rest of day at leisure.

Days 7–8 Morning, drive to Mirissa Fisheries Harbour and board the boat to search for whales. Blue and Sperm Whales are both seen regularly in these waters. On more than 500 whale watches in the first four years, during the season, the Blue Whales have had an encounter rate of over 90 per cent.

Day 9 After breakfast, leave for Negombo for one night. Rest of the day at leisure by the beach.

Day 10 Transfer to international airport. Tour ends.

Ultimate Island Safari (12 nights/13 days)

As discussed earlier, Sri Lanka is unmatched for its wildlife for an island of its size, and it has a host of biodiversity-rich features and beautiful landscapes.

Day 1 Arrive in Sri Lanka and transfer to Galle for three nights. Remainder of the day at leisure.

Day 2 Morning, drive to Mirissa Fisheries Harbour and board boat to search for whales. Blue and Sperm Whales are both seen regularly in these waters. On a good day you may also be treated to more than 500 Spinner Dolphins. Spend the rest of the day at leisure or explore the Dutch-built Galle Dutch Fort (a UNESCO World Heritage Site).

Day 3 After breakfast leave to Yala for three nights. Yala is one of the best national parks in the world and one of the top two parks in Asia (together with Corbett in India) for seeing mammals. A few game drives can yield the Asian Elephant, Leopard, Sloth Bear, Golden

Jackal, Sambar, Spotted Deer, Hanuman Langur, Toque Macaque, Ruddy and Stripe-necked Mongooses, Wild Pig, Palm and Giant Squirrels, and Black-naped Hare. The public roads leading to the park can in the night yield the Jungle Cat, Common Palm-civet, Ring-tailed Civet and Indian Gerbil (*Tatera indica*). The park has an abundance of bird life and is also a good place for butterflies.

Days 4–5 Morning and afternoon game drives in Yala National Park, with emphasis on elephant, Leopard and Sloth Bear.

Day 6 After breakfast, leave to Sinharaja for two nights. Afternoon, explore the rainforest in search of the bird wave. Birding highlights include endemics such as the Red-faced Malkoha, Ceylon Blue Magpie, White-faced Starling and Scaly Thrush.

Day 7 Morning and afternoon walks in rainforest in search of bird waves and other endemic fauna, including dragonflies, butterflies and lizards, and flora.

Day 8 After breakfast leave to Nuwara Eliya for two nights. En route, visit ancient monastic ruins of Buduruvagala. Pause at Ella Gap for landscape photography. Remainder of the day at leisure.

Day 9 Morning visit to Horton Plains National Park, for montane endemics and superb landscapes. Horton Plains is famous for World's End, a stunning viewpoint that is a sheer drop of 870 m (2,854 ft) hidden in clouds. In addition to cloud forests there are open grasslands on the lower slopes that serve as feeding grounds for herbivores such as Sambar. In the forest patches look for the endemic Bear Monkey and Dusky-striped Squirrel. Look for montane endemic birds such as the Yellow-eared Bulbul, Sri Lanka Bush-warbler (*Bradypterus palliseri*), Ceylon Wood Pigeon, Ceylon Hill White-eye, Dusky-blue Flycatcher and, if lucky, the crepuscular endemic Ceylon Whistling-thrush. Afterwards, visit Hakgala Botanical Gardens for the montane races of the Purple-faced leaf Monkey and Toque Monkey. Both are habituated and permit photography. More opportunities for montane birds.

Day 10 After breakfast, leave to Habarana for two nights. En route stop over in Kandy and visit the sacred Temple of the Tooth.

Day 11 Early morning, visit the ancient city of Polonnaruwa, a UNESCO archaeological site, to watch troops of the dry lowland race of the Toque Monkey, the northern race of the Purple-faced Leaf Monkey and the Hanuman Langur. Afternoon, during the season, visit the Minneriya National Park to witness the Elephant Gathering.

Day 12 After breakfast, leave to Negombo for one night. En route to Negombo, visit the ancient Dambulla Rock Temple.

Day 13 Transfer to International Airport.

Birding Holiday (13 nights/14 days)

For an island of its size, Sri Lanka has a high species density of birds. As stated earlier, about 450 birds have been recorded, including migrants. No less than 33 species of bird are endemic (the full list of endemic species is listed on page 198). The mixed-species feeding flocks in Sinharaja are the largest in the world.

Day 1 Arrive in Sri Lanka and transfer to Colombo for one night. Afternoon, walk in Talangama Wetland to look for Black and Yellow Bitterns, Watercock and some common birds such as the Pheasant-tailed Jacana and Purple Coot.

Day 2 Morning, drive to Bodhinagala Forest Reserve, a lowland rainforest closer to Colombo. Look for the Ceylon Grey Hornbill, Yellow-fronted Barbet, Ceylon Hanging-parrot and, if lucky, the scarce endemic Green-billed Coucal. Thereafter proceed to Sinharaja for three nights.

Days 3–4 Early-morning and late-afternoon walks in Sinharaja Rainforest for lowland endemics and mixed-species bird flocks. Birding highlights include the Red-faced Malkoha, Ceylon Blue Magpie, White-faced Starling and Ceylon Scaly Thrush.

Day 5 After breakfast, leave for Uda Walawe for one night. Afternoon, game drive at Uda Walawe National Park for dry-zone birding and the Asian Elephant. Uda Walawe is the only park in the world where a wild elephant sighting is guaranteed. For birders, it is one of the country's top spots for watching birds of prey. Look for the Grey-headed Fishing Eagle, Black-shouldered Kite, Changeable Hawk Eagle, Crested Serpent Eagle,

White-bellied Sea Eagle, Shikra, Common Kestrel, Brown Fish-owl and Western Marsh Harrier. Also look for the Malabar Pied Hornbill, Thick-billed Flowerpecker, Plum-headed Parakeet, Common Hoopoe, Sirkeer Malkoha, Blue-faced Malkoha, Little Green Bee-eater, Barred Buttonquail (*Turnix suscitator leggei*), Indian Silverbill (*Lonchura malabarica malabarica*) and Black-headed Munia (*Lonchura malacca*), and for the migrants, which include the Black-capped Purple Kingfisher (*Halcyon pileata*), Blyth's Pipit (*Anthus godlewskii*) and Orange-headed Thrush (*Zoothera citrina citrina*).

Day 6 Early morning, one last safari in Uda Walawe for dry-zone specialties. After breakfast leave for Yala for three nights. Afternoon birding at Palatupana Saltpans for shorebirds. Waders during the migrant season include the Ruddy Turnstone (*Arenaria interpres interpres*), Little Ringed Plover (*Charadrius dubius*), Kentish, Lesser Sand, Greater Sand, Grey and Golden Plovers, Little Stint, Curlew, Common and Marsh Sandpipers, and Common Redshank. In the open patches you may see the odd-looking Great and Eurasian Thick-knees, and the Ashy-crowned Sparrow Lark (*Eremopterix grisea*).

Day 7 Morning and afternoon game drive in Yala National Park for dry-zone birding. A day's birding in the park during the northern winter can yield as many as 100 species. Look out for dry-zone specialties like Eurasian and Great Thick-knees, Sirkeer and Blue-faced Malkohas and Malabar Pied Hornbills. In the park's numerous waterholes the Painted Stork, Lesser Whistling-duck, Black-headed Ibis, Eurasian Spoonbill, Great Egret, Median Egret (*Mesophoyx intermedia intermedia*), Little Egret (*Egretta garzetta*) and rare Black-necked Stork may be seen. Also keep a lookout for endemics such as the Ceylon Swallow, Ceylon Wood-Shrike and Ceylon Junglefowl. Yala is excellent for watching larger animals including the Leopard, Sloth Bear, Asian Elephant, Mugger Crocodile, Sambar and Golden Jackal.

Day 8 Early-morning game drive in nearby Bundala National Park. Among the larger waterbirds you could see are the Lesser Adjutant, Painted Stork, Asian Openbill, Eurasian Spoonbill, Black-headed Ibis and Woolly-necked Stork (*Ciconia episcopus episcopus*), and many species of wader during the northern winter. Afternoon, one last safari in Yala for birding and other wildlife.

Day 9 After breakfast leave for Nuwara Eliya for two nights. Afternoon visit to Victoria Park for Himalayan migrants such as the Kashmir Flycatcher, Pied Thrush (*Zoothera wardii*), Indian Pitta and Indian Blue Robin. Endemics include the Yellow-eared Bulbul, Ceylon Hill White-eye and Dusky-blue Flycatcher. Also visit the nearby Elephant Nook wetland at one end of Lake Gregory for the proposed endemic Black-throated Munia or Ceylon Hill Munia, Paddyfield Pipit (*Anthus rufulus malayensis*), Pied Bush Chat, Pintail Snipe, Zitting Cisticola (*Cisticola juncidis*), Plain Prinia (*Prinia inornata insularis*), Blyth's Reed Warbler (*Acrocephalus dumetorum*) and, if lucky, Pallas's Grasshopper Warbler (*Locustella naevia*).

Day 10 Morning, visit Horton Plains National Park for montane endemics and superb landscapes. Horton Plains is famous for World's End, a stunning viewpoint, which is a sheer drop of 870 m (2,854 ft). In addition to cloud forests there are also open grasslands on the lower slopes, which serve as feeding grounds for herbivores such as the Sambar. In the forest patches look for the northern race of the endemic Purple-faced Leaf Monkey (the Bear Monkey) and Dusky-striped Squirrel. Look for montane endemics such as the Yellow-eared Bulbul, Ceylon Bush-warbler, Ceylon Wood Pigeon, Ceylon Hill White-eye, Dusky-blue Flycatcher and, if lucky, the scarce montane endemic the Ceylon Whistling-thrush. Afterwards, visit Hakgala Botanical Gardens for habituated Purple-faced Leaf Monkeys and a chance to see montane birds.

Day 11 After breakfast, leave for Kithulgala for two nights. Afternoon, cross the Kelani River in a dugout canoe and reach the Kelani Valley Forest Reserve, a lowland tropical rainforest rich in endemic fauna and flora. The reserve is ideal for any lowland endemics and provides another chance to see the Ceylon Hill Myna, Green-billed Coucal, Spot-winged Thrush, Ceylon Blue Magpie, Ceylon Spurfowl, Brown-capped

Babbler and Red-faced Malkoha.
Day 12 Morning and afternoon, endemic birding in Kelani Valley Forest Reserve.
Day 13 After breakfast, leave for Waikkal. Late-afternoon boat trip in Waikkal for waterbirds. Highlights include Black, Yellow and Cinnamon (*Ixobrychus cinnamomeus*) Bitterns, Little Green Herons (*Butorides striatus*) and the migrant Black-capped Purple Kingfisher.
Day 14 Transfer to International Airport.

Checklists of Endemic Birds and Mammals

In the interests of space the lists of endemic species have been restricted to the birds, mammals and butterflies (see page 78), which are the most popular animal groups with visitors to Sri Lanka.

Endemic Birds

Galliformes
Partridges, quails and pheasants (Phasianidae)
1. Ceylon Spurfowl (*Galloperdix bicalcarata*)
2. Ceylon Junglefowl (*Gallus lafayetii*)

Columbiformes
Pigeons and doves (Columbidae)
3. Ceylon Wood Pigeon (*Columba torringtonii*)
4. Ceylon Green-pigeon (*Treron pompadora*)

Psittaciformes
Parrots (Psittacidae)
5. Ceylon Hanging-parrot (*Loriculus beryllinus*)
6. Layard's Parakeet (*Psittacula calthropae*)

Cuculiformes
Cuckoos (*Cuculidae*)
7. Green-billed Coucal (*Centropus chlororhynchos*)
8. Red-faced Malkoha (*Phaenicophaeus pyrrhocephalus*)

Strigiformes
Owls (Strigidae)
9. Serendib Scops-owl (*Otus thilohoffmanni*)
10. Chestnut-backed Owlet (*Glaucidium castanonotum*)

Coraciiformes
Hornbills (Bucerotidae)
11. Ceylon Grey Hornbill (*Ocyceros gingalensis*)

Piciformes
Barbets (Capitonidae)
12. Yellow-fronted Barbet (*Megalaima flavifrons*)
13. Ceylon Small Barbet (*Megalaima rubricapillus*)

Woodpeckers (Picidae)
14. Greater Flameback (*Chrysocolaptes stricklandi*)

Passeriformes
Swallows and martins (Hirundinidae)
15. Ceylon Swallow (*Hirundo hyperythra*)

Cuckooshrikes (Campephagidae)
16. Ceylon Wood-Shrike (*Tephrodornis affinis*)

Bulbuls (Pycnonotidae)
17. Black-capped Bulbul (*Pycnonotus melanicterus*)
18. Yellow-eared Bulbul (*Pycnonotus penicillatus*)

Thrushes (Turdidae)
19. Spot-winged Thrush (*Zoothera spiloptera*)
20. Ceylon Scaly Thrush (*Zoothera imbricata*)
21. Ceylon Whistling-thrush (*Myophonus blighi*)

Old World flycatchers and chats (Muscicapidae)
22. Dusky-blue Flycatcher (*Eumyias sordidus*)

Babblers (Timaliidae)
23. Ashy-headed Laughingthrush (*Garrulax cinereifrons*)
24. Brown-capped Babbler (*Pellorneum fuscocapillus*)
25. Ceylon Scimitar Babbler (*Pomatorhinus* [*schisticeps*] *melanurus*)

26. Ceylon Rufous Babbler (*Turdoides rufescens*)

Old World warblers (Sylviidae)
27. Sri Lanka Bush-warbler (*Elaphrornis palliseri*)

Flowerpeckers (Dicaeidae)
28. Legge's Flowerpecker (*Dicaeum vincens*)

White-eyes (Zosteropidae)
29. Ceylon Hill White-eye (*Zosterops ceylonensis*)

Starlings and mynas (Sturnidae)
30. White-faced Starling (*Sturnia albofrontata*)
31. Ceylon Hill Myna (*Gracula ptilogenys*)

Drongos (Dicruridae)
32. Ceylon Crested Drongo (*Dicrurus lophorinus*)

Crows, jays, magpies and treepies (Corvidae)
33. Ceylon Blue Magpie (*Urocissa ornata*)

Above: *The Sri Lanka Bush-warbler is heard more than seen in thickets of* Strobilanthes.

Endemic Mammals

Insectivora

Shrews (Soricidae)

1. Ceylon Long-tailed Shrew (*Crocidura miya*)
2. Sinharaja Shrew (*Crocidura hikmiya*)
3. Kelaart's Long-clawed Shrew (*Feroculus feroculus*)
4. Pearson's Long-clawed Shrew (*Solisorex pearsoni*)
5. Ceylon Shrew (*Suncus zeylanicus*)
6. Sri Lanka Pigmy Shrew (*Suncus fellowesgordoni*)

Primates

Lorises (Lorisidae)

7. Red Slender Loris (*Loris tardigradus*)

Monkeys (Cercopithecidae)

8. Toque Macaque (*Macaca sinica*)
9. Purple-faced Leaf Monkey (*Semnopithecus vetulus*)

Carnivora

Civets (Viverridae)

10. Golden Wet-zone Palm Civet (*Paradoxurus aureus*)
11. Sri Lankan Brown Palm Civet (*Paradoxurus montanus*)
12. Golden Dry-zone Palm Civet (*Paradoxurus stenocephalus*)

Artiodactyla

Mouse-deer (Tragulidae)

13. White-spotted Chevrotain (*Tragulus meminna*)
14. Yellow-striped Chevrotain (*Tragulus kathygre*)

Rodentia

Giant, Tree, Ground and Flying Squirrels (Sciuridae)

15. Layard's Striped Squirrel (*Funambulus layardi*)
16. Ceylon Dusky-striped Squirrel (*Funambulus obscurus*)

Rats and Mice (Muridae)

17. Fernando's Mouse (*Mus fernandoni*)
18. Sri Lanka Spiny Mouse (*Mus mayori*)
19. Montane Rat (*Rattus montanus*)
20. Ohiya Rat (*Srilankamys ohiensis*)
21. Long-tailed Tree Mouse (*Vandeleuria nolthenii*)

Right: *The mid-stripe of the endemic Layard's Striped Squirrel can be vivid in the low-lit forests.*

Bibliography

Birds

de Silva Wijeyeratne, G. (2009). *Birds of Sri Lanka.* National Trust – Sri Lanka: Colombo.

de Silva Wijeyeratne, G., Warakagoda, D. and de Zylva, Dr T. S. U. (2000). *A Photographic Guide to the Birds of Sri Lanka.* New Holland: London.

Harrison, J. (2011). *A Field Guide to the Birds of Sri Lanka.* 2nd edn. Oxford University Press: Oxford.

Henry, G. M. (1998). *A Guide to the Birds of Ceylon.* 3rd revised edn. Oxford University Press: India.

Kotagama, S., and Fernando, P. (1994). *A Field Guide to the Birds of Sri Lanka.* Wildlife Heritage Trust: Colombo.

Warakagoda, D., Inskipp, C., Inskipp, T. and Grimmet, R. (2012). *Birds of Sri Lanka.* Helm Field Guides. Christopher Helm: London.

Butterflies

Banks, J. and Banks, J. (1985, several reprints). *A Selection of the Butterflies of Sri Lanka.* Lake House Investments: Colombo.

d'Abrera, B. (1998). *The Butterflies of Ceylon.* Wildlife Heritage Trust: Colombo.

de Silva Wijeyeratne, G. (2006). *Butterflies of Sri Lanka and Southern India.* Gehan's Photo Booklet Series. Jetwing Eco Holidays: Colombo.

Haribal, M. (1992). *The Butterflies of Sikkim Himalaya and their Natural History.* Natraj Publishers: Dehra Dun.

Kunte, K. (2000). *India – A Lifescape: Butterflies of Peninsular India.* Universities Press (India) Limited: India.

Dragonflies

Bedjanič, Matjaž, de Silva Wijeyeratne, G. and Conniff, K. (2006). *Dragonflies of Sri Lanka and Southern India.* Gehan's Photo Booklet Series. 1st edn. Eco Holidays: Colombo.

de Fonseka, T. (2000). *The Dragonflies of Sri Lanka.* Wildlife Heritage Trust: Colombo.

Fish

Pethiyagoda R. (1991). *Freshwater Fishes of Sri Lanka.* Wildlife Heritage Trust: Sri Lanka.

Mammals

de Silva Wijeyeratne, G. (2008). *A Photographic Guide to Mammals of Sri Lanka.* New Holland: London.

Phillips, W. W. A. (1980). *Manual of the Mammals of Sri Lanka.* 2nd revised edn. Wildlife and Nature Protection Society of Sri Lanka: Colombo.

Reptiles

Das, I. and de Silva, A. (2005). *A Photographic Guide to Snakes and other Reptiles of Sri Lanka.* New Holland: London.

Somaweera, R. and Somaweera, N. (2009). *Lizards of Sri Lanka: A Colour Guide with Field Keys.* Chimaira Buchhandelsgesellschaft mbH: Germany.

General Wildlife

de Silva Wijeyeratne, G. (2007). *Sri Lankan Wildlife.* Bradt Travel Guides: UK.

de Silva Wijeyeratne, G. (ed.) (2004). *Leopards & Other Wildlife of Yala.* Eco Holidays: Colombo.

Pethiyagoda, R. (1998). *Ours to Protect Sri Lanka's Biodiversity Heritage.* Publications (Pvt.) Limited: Colombo.

Vigallon, S. (2007). *The Sinharaja Guidebook for Eco-tourists.* Stamford Lake Publications: Columbo.

Marine Wildlife

Anderson, C. A. (1996). *Common Reef Fishes of Sri Lanka.* Wildlife Heritage Trust of Sri Lanka: Collumbo.

Cresswell, C., Walker, D. and T. Pusser (2007). *Whales & Dolphins of the North American Pacific.* Wild Guides Ltd: UK.

Walker, D. and Creswell, G. (2011). *Whales and Dolphins of the European Atlantic: The Bay of Biscay, English Channel, Celtic Sea and Coastal SW Ireland.* Wild Guides Ltd: UK.

Ilangakoon, A. (2002). *Whales & Dolphins Sri Lanka.* WHT Publications (Private) Ltd: Colombo.

Shirihai, H. and Jarrett, B. (2006). *Whales, Dolphins and Seals. A Field Guide to the Marine Mammals of the World.* A&C Black Publishers: London.

Jefferson, T. A., Webber, M. A., Pitman, R. L. and Brett Jarrett (2008). *Marine Mammals of the World: A Comprehensive Guide to their Identification.* Academic Press.

Onley, D., Scofield, P. (2007). *Albatrosses, Petrels and Shearwaters of the World.* Helm Field Guides. Christopher Helm: London.

Rice, W. D. (1988). *Marine Mammals of the World: Systematics and Distribution.* Special Publication No. 4. The Society for Marine Mammalogy: USA.

Soper, T., Powell, D. (2008). *Wildlife of the North Atlantic.* Bradt Travel Guides: UK.

Key Article References

Big Game and General Wildlife

de Silva Wijeyeratne, G. (2010). 'Our big five. Why Sri Lanka is the best for big game safaris outside Africa'. *The Sunday Times Plus.* 18 October 2010. http://sundaytimes.lk/101017/Plus/plus_23.html

de Silva Wijeyeratne, G. (2010). 'Sri Lanka's big five'. *Hi Magazine.* Series 8, vol. 2. September 2010. pp. 198–202.

de Silva Wijeyeratne, G. (2009). 'Leopard safaris. How the Leopard's spots were changed to eco dollars'. *Hi Magazine.* March 2009. Series 7, vol. 1. pp. 154–6.

de Silva Wijeyeratne, G. (2008). 'The Gathering – a billion rupees of elephants'. *Hi Magazine.* December 2008. Series 6, vol. 5. pp. 202–204.

Marine Wildlife

de Silva Wijeyeratne, G. (2012). 'Sri Lanka Best Chance for Sperm Whale Super-pods'. *Sunday Times: Sri Lanka. The Sunday Times Plus.* 5 August 2012. p. 6.

de Silva Wijeyeratne, G. (2011). 'Longest and best for Blue'. *The Sunday Times Plus.* 4 September 2011. p. 6. sundaytimes.lk/110904/Plus/plus_08.html

de Silva Wijeyeratne, G. (2010). 'Off to see seabirds'. *The Sunday Times Plus.* 2 May 2010. p. 6. www.sundaytimes.lk/100502/Plus/plus_15.html

de Silva Wijeyeratne, G. (2010). 'Why Kalpitiya is Sri Lanka's top spot for pelagic seabirds'. *Hi Magazine.* Series 8, vol. 1. pp. 228–31. www.wildlifeextra.com/go/birds/asian-pelagics.html

de Silva Wijeyeratne, G. (2010). 'Kalpitiya joins Sri Lanka's whale spots'. *The Sunday Times Plus.* 7 March 2010. p. 4. www.sundaytimes.lk/100307/Plus/plus_13.html

de Silva Wijeyeratne, G. (2009). 'Best for Blue – one year on'. *Serendib,* the in-flight magazine of Sri Lanka. November–December 2009. pp. 50–53.

de Silva Wijeyeratne, G. (2008). 'Best of Blue'. *Serendib,* the in-flight magazine of Sri Lanka. November–December 2008. pp. 42–6.

de Silva Wijeyeratne, G. (2008). 'Best for Blue. Is Sri Lanka the world's top spot for seeing Blue and Sperm Whales?'. May 2008. Open Release Article.

Biodiversity

de Silva Wijeyeratne, G. (2013). 'A winner in the wilds'. *The Sunday Times Plus.* 13 January 2013. p.3. www.sundaytimes.lk/130113/plus/a-winner-in-the-wilds-28039.html

de Silva Wijeyeratne, G. (2010). 'Butterfly safaris: the development of photographic guides'. *Hi Magazine.* Series 8, vol. 3. pp. 242–3.

de Silva Wijeyeratne, G. (2009). 'The Sinharaja bird wave'. *Hi Magazine.* May 2009. Series 7, vol. 2. pp. 146–7.

de Silva Wijeyeratne, G. (2009). 'The Dragons of Lanka'. *Hi Magazine.* August 2009. Series 7, vol. 3. pp. 182–3.

Acknowledgements

General acknowledgements

My efforts to publicize Sri Lanka and its wildlife were made possible by the support of many people in Sri Lanka's tourism and wildlife conservation sectors. Past and present staff of the Jetwing (Eco Holidays, Hotels and Travels) including Chandrika Maelge, Amila

Salgado, Ajanthan Shantiratnam, Paramie Perera, Nadeeshani Attanayake, Ganganath Weerasinghe, Riaz Cader, Ayanthi Samarajewa, Shehani Seneviratne, Aruni Hewage, Divya Martyn, L. S. de S Gunasekera, Chadraguptha Wickremesekera ('Wicky'), Supurna Hettiarachchi ('Hetti'), Chaminda Jayaweera , Sam Caseer, Chandra Jayawardana, Nadeera Weerasinghe, Anoma Alagiyawadu, Hasantha Lokugamage 'Basha', Wijaya Bandara, Suranga Wewegedara, Prashantha Paranagama, Nilantha Kodithuwakku, Dithya Angammana, Asitha Jayaratne, Lal de Silva, Hiran Cooray, Shiromal Cooray, Ruan Samarasinha, Raju Arasaratnam, Sanjiva Gautamadasa and Lalin de Mel and several others have helped in numerous ways. Hiran and Shiromal Cooray in their wider role as business leaders in Sri Lanka supported my efforts to chase the big stories.

The field staff of the Department of Wildlife Conservation and Forest Department, naturalist guides, safari-vehicle drivers and many others have accompanied me in the field and shared their knowledge and experience. Others in tourism who have helped me include Chitral Jayatilake and his colleagues at John Keells, Dallas Martenstyn (Bar Reef Resort & Dolphin Beach), Anuruddha Bandara (EcoTeam) and Ashan Seneviratne (Little Adventures). Many scientists have inspired me, including Rohan Pethiyagoda, Dr Dinarzarde Raheem, Professor Anna Nekaris, Dr Karen Conniff, Matjaž Bedjanič and Dr Charles Anderson. Azly Nazeem, Jeevan William, Lester Perera and my former scout master Mr Lokanathan were key early influences.

My late mother Lakshmi encouraged me to read and write. Editors of various publications whose encouragement I have received include Hiran Hewavisenthi and his team in LMD and LIVING, Krishan Senaratne and Arlaka Jayasekera (*Serendipity*), Shyamalee Tudawe (*Hi Magazine*) and several of the editorial staff from the local newspapers, including Renuka Sadananthan (*Sunday Times*) and Hiranthi Fernando (*Funday Times*) and many presenters, producers and camera crew, such as Asantha Sirimane and Charitha Fernando from Vanguard.

I could not have got this far if it were not for the support of my late parents Dalton and Lakshmi de Silva Wijeyeratne, my Uncle Dodwell de Silva, my late Aunt Vijitha de Silva and my brother and sisters. My Uncle Dodwell de Silva sparked my interest in wildlife and photography, and my late Aunt Vijita de Silva and sister Manouri gave me my first cameras. My sisters Indira, Manouri, Janani, Rukshan, Dileeni and Yasmin, and brother Suraj, have always supported and encouraged me. In the UK, my sister Indira and her family (Kingsley, Sashini, Janek and Ruwan) provide a home when I am bridging islands.

Specific acknowledgements

Tara Wikramanayake has assisted me by proofreading many of the things I write, including this book. Georgina Gemmell assisted Tara and me in filling in the Latin names for many species. My thanks to John Beaufoy, Rosemary Wilkinson (project manager), Krystyna Mayer (editor), Glyn Bridgewater (designer) and others on the John Beaufoy Publishing team.

The editors of *Priority Magazine* (Publicitas Publishing), *American Birding, Alula, Hi Magazine* and *The Sunday Times* (Sri Lanka) kindly permitted me to adapt articles first published with them. Geoffrey Dobbs agreed to a future guide to whale watching and the rainforests of Galle to be written with extracts for use in this book. Jetwing Eco Holidays allowed me to adapt the structure of their client-tested itineraries. Riaz Cader, Chitral Jayatilake, Ashan Seneviratne, Ranil Nanayakkara, Lalith Ekanayake and Aruna Seneviratne answered various questions, especially in relation to the wildlife calendar.

My wife Nirma and my two daughters Maya and Amali put up with me not spending the time with them they deserve because of my taking natural history to a wider audience. Nirma, at times with help from her parents Roland and Neela Silva, takes care of many things, small and large, to look after a family.

The people and organizations who have helped are too long to mention individually and those mentioned here are only representative. To those whom I have not mentioned by name – your support did matter.

Index

T

U

V

W

X

Y

Z

First published in the United Kingdom in 2013 by
John Beaufoy Publishing,
11 Blenheim Court, 316 Woodstock Road,
Oxford OX2 7NS, U.K.
www.johnbeaufoy.com

10 9 8 7 6 5 4 3 2 1

ISBN 978-1-906780-98-2

Edited by Krystyna Mayer
Designed by Glyn Bridgewater
Cartography by William Smuts
Project management by Rosemary Wilkinson
Printed and bound in Singapore by Tien Wah Press (Pte) Ltd.